CLEAR!

Dennis R. Blocker II

Dedication

I dedicate this book to the hundreds of amazing Nurses, Medics, Clerks, Doctors, PA's, Admins and Ancillary Staff who taught me so much over two decades of my life.

Together we experienced an astounding range of human events and emotions. We mourned the loss of dear friends who'd faithfully stood beside us on the front lines. Yet, other times the air was filled with laughter as coworkers pranked and cracked jokes. Then, in somber silence, we delicately washed the mangled lifeless bodies of strangers and somehow remained sane. Though we were assaulted by smells and patients alike, we kept coming back for more. Why? Because our friends were there, and there were lives to save.

To you, my friends and coworkers, this book is dedicated.

Trauma Center

Leadership:

Jim Martin (RIP) – Rose D. – Kathy T. – Pablo R. – Denise D. – Rose B. – Ernest P. – Rebecca S. – Becky R. – Eloise (RIP)

Doctors:

Dr. Arkangel – Dr. W. Harrison – Dr. Bauer – Dr. Morale – Dr. Williams – Dr. Nieto – Dr. Grijalva – Dr. Hnatow – Dr. Spitz – Dr. "My Eye!" – Dr. Glendenning – Dr. Rezaie – Dr. Stewart – Dr. Myers – Dr. Latham – Dr. Savage – Dr. Dent – Dr. Cornei

Physician Assistants:

Bob G. "US Navy" – Peter F. "US Army" – Jose P. "Army Green Beret" – Mark S. "US Army" – Ron D. "Army Green Beret" – Doug G. "US Army Ranger" – John K.– Greg G. "US Army" – Larry W. "US Army" – Terry E. – Jerald W. "US Army" – Ken G. "US Army" – Steve S. "US Army" – Ingrid C. – Krista

Nurses:

Chris E., – Jennifer Pfeffer "Sis" – Misty D. – Tim F. – Denise E. – Will H. – Melissa T. – Chrissi M. – Lindsey R. – Simon Fonseca Jr. "RIP Brother" – Marla K. – Shawna A. L – Tom C. – April E. – Candy L. Cora S. – Emma C. – Shawn H. – Joann H. – Vergie – Cici M. – Rosemary P. – Bre G. – Javine A. – Tony I. Laura G. "My Faithful Supporter" – Mauricio S. – Noemi G. – Cindy H. – Janet B. – Hector R. – Angie C. – Yuri Z. – Tami H. – Kristy O. N. – Nancy G. – Elsie H. – Gina H. – Jennifer J. "Flight Nurse" – Darlene N. Sandy F. – Jodi M. – Sharon A. – Tracy F. – Lisa P. – Lauren W. – Vanessa B. – Kornelia T. – Patti B. – Celia B. – Holly L. – Lou Ann M. Sherri D. – Darrin M. "Rainbow" – Priscilla B. – Rick M. – Ivonne D. – Traci U. – Janie D. – Cindy R. – Sarah S. M. – Tonna G. Lee R. G. – Sheila G. – Monica E. – Emma C. – Peggy S. – Neil D. – Tabitha – Kerri D. – Susan W. – Alex – Christian B. – Sabine B. – Heath – Tina – Teresa R. – Mitch V. – Pam G. – Ivonne D.

Medics/ER Techs:

Lorenzo R. – Dino L. "US Army Paratrooper" – Mike D. (Now an RN) – Rudy J. (Now an RN) – Keri M. – Eddie E. – Lorann P. – Maria "The Tuche!" – Mike R. – Barbara W. "My EMT Preceptor" – Dean E. "My Renaissance Fest. Buddy" – Don C. – Renee V. (Now an RN) – Yvette P. (Now an RN) – Geoff S. – Steve V. – Bernardo (Now an RN) – Matt L. – CJ – Philip D. L. S. (Now a Nurse Practitioner) – Jesus B., (Now a PA) – Steven B. "US Army" – Armando O. (Now an RN) – Lulu G. B. – Crispin H. – Rick S. (Now an RN) – Tom L. – Roger D. "US Army" (Now an RN)

Clerks:

Lisa R. – Elaine G. – Pam C. – Henry R. – Melinda – Katharine C. – Lannie V. – Rosalie G. – MariJo

Ancillary:

Mike P. "X-ray" – Mylissa M. "CT" – Allen A. "RT" – Greg E. "Registration" – Judy W. "CT" – Rosalie G. – Jackie "CT" – Erin V. "Social Worker" – Annette E. "Registration" – Regina R.M. – Jaime M. "Registration" – Maria G. "Registration"

Second ER

Leadership:

Kara K. – Denise D. – Rose D. – Sandy D. – Gilliam C. – Stacie M. – Kevin K.

Doctors:

Dr. Romo "My Benefactor" – Dr. Harrison – Dr. Schuster

Nurses:

Natalie Mike - "Blocker you better get these people squared away!"
Kevin Trainor - "Dennis just fell in the glacier water run off!"

Arnold P. – Pura - David M. "Falcor!" - Ashley B. - Dena K. - Stefanie D. - Adrienne L. - Christi L. - Lacey S. - Kelly W. - Erin M. - Marisol S. - Victoria S. - Jessica T. - Jessie T. - Laura O. - Melissa M. - Jessica D. G. - Jessie M. - Angelo R. - Angie

Medics/ER Techs:

Chad B. - Joonoh (Now an RN) - Michelle A. (Now an RN) - Erik D. R. - Paul Delagarza (Now flight medic) - Matt (Now an RN) – Dwayne - Cindy

Clerks:

Leah B. - Jody W. - Connie "How was Woodstock?"

Ancillary:

Michael O "The Pharmacist" - Adrienne J. "Registration" - Roxanne B. G. "Registration" – Jessica D. "Radiology"

Third ER

Leadership:

Miriam - Sam C. - Corryn K. - Kim L. - Shari B. - Melissa L.

Doctors:

Dr. Mehta - Dr. Williams - Dr. Rezaie - Dr. Gemmill - Dr. Meyer - Dr. Julien - Dr. Mandizzle - Dr. Nugent Dr. Boothby - Dr. Black - Dr. Cromwell - Dr. Hnatow - Dr. Esaep - Dr. Frolichstein - Dr. Chopra – Dr. Schuster - Dr. Wilson - Dr. Stephens - Dr. Lillich - Dr. Dillon - Dr. Spitz

Physician Assistants:

Amara W. – Courtney G. – Kelsey M. – Zach T.,

Nurse Practitioners:

Paula M. – Kristina B. "Bulgarian Bomb Shell" – Chris G. – Jody M. – Stacy N.,

Charge Nurses:

Alexa Salinas-Ferris – Damaris Cisneros – Branda P. — Sarah — Sam – Shawn L. — Bryce C.

Nurses:

Sandy B. – Jaycee A. – Kim Z. "Go Pack" – Stephen G. – Chelsea F. – Brian R. – Kaitlyn B. – Elana S. — Mio – David T. – Allison H. – David N. – Sarah P. — Karizza – Heather D. – Terrie H. – Crystal S. – Norchel Jessica S. – Hannah W. – Sarah M. C. – Brooke P. — Camille — Narges – Sara W. K. – Haley C. – Karen B. Cornelius W. – Will P. – Jennifer F. – Faith R. – Emilie M. – Bryce C. – Shawn L. – Chris J. — Leigh — Amber – Lori J. – Philip C. – Amanda R. –   Jake – Nisha K. – Traceen "L.T." — Megan S. – Sinead M. — Paul R. – Scott G. – Stephaine E. – Rick N. – Adam D. — Monica – Kelley P. – Adrian M. – Red Beard — Livy G. — Becky S. –

Medics/ER Techs:

Andrew Warren – Steve S. — Armando — Alex – Stephanie "The Padawan/Work Daughter" – Robert G. Dan – Cody (Now an RN) – Vanessa R. (Now an RN) — Shandle – Cisco – Blake H. – Chris T. — Shannon H (now an RN) – Victoria C. (Now an RN) – James – Ashley — Jacob — Smitty – Megan S. — Suzy Jared – Dennis R. (Now an RN) – Nikki N. (LOL)

The Old Men (Medics)

Patrick "Patty Melt" Soto (US Army) – Mike Talamantes (USMC / US Army retired)

The Clerks:

Juvona J. - Emily G. — Ariel - Cynthia T. - Lonnie

Ancillary:

Rick G. "The Lab" - DeAnna "The Pharmacist" - Lee S. "EMS Liaison" Patty T. — Jessica "The Pharmacist" Danyl Cantu "CT" - James W. - Tiffany L. M. "Registration" - Michelle H.

Special Mention:

Rudy (The Labrador Retriever PTSD Dog)

Table of Contents

Dedication	3
Acknowledgements	13
Introduction	15

Part One – Molding   **21**

Dead Man's Hill	22
Smoke Spires	29
Nothings Gonna Happen	34
Taxi Service	47
A Woman Scorned	53
Last Door on the Right	60
A Bridge, a Seat, and a Dilemma	73
Charley	87
The Alphas	101
The Nam	107
Triage	109
Learning Curve	122
Bridges	129

Part Two – Trauma.   **134**

Comfortable	135
The Lawsuit	136
Hammer Time	137
Down Mexico Way	138
Tough Customers	147
The Nursing Home	153
White Foam	155
The Jedi	158
A Visit from Spider Man	161
Emergency Fast Food	164
He'll be Back	168
Rescue Mission…Wait…What?	171
Long Blonde Hair	174
Angels and Demons	176

The Veterans	190
They All Run Together	198
The Bear	213
Memorial Day Weekend	220
The Dark Passenger	234

Part Three – Dire Straits   **242**

A New ER	243
Tough Guy Tears	249
The Streak	253
Somewhere in Time	256
A Case for Experience	262
A Village	272
Saving a Doc	275
Twins	283
Time to Move on…Again	287
Ups and Downs	289
Do I Care?	297
Countdown	303
The Shrink	316
Cross Country	331
Broken Glass	338
Go Pack!	349
Clear!	355

Acknowledgments

This book would not have been possible without the recommendation from my father that I put my memories down for all to read. Hearing the myriad of stories locked in my brain, my father felt that folks would really benefit from their transfer to paper.

I also owe a great debt of gratitude to Katie Geisler Richards who, with patience and grace, listened to me read every single word that I had typed. This was a long process that involved many rewrites, and she was there during all of them. I laugh when I recall our thirty-minute conversations regarding the placement of a punctuation mark. I loved every minute of it.

I also wish to thank my mother, sisters, nephews, niece, and daughters Lauren and Brooke, who listened to me read the stories as they were finished. Your input was invaluable.

The encouragement of my longtime friend and sister Jennifer Pfeffer (RN) was a huge boon to my efforts. We've been through a lot together and served in the same trenches.

Thank you to my paramedic buddy Andrew Warren for casting a knowing eye on the manuscript. His twenty years of experience as a Paramedic were greatly coveted and thus his input invaluable.

I wish to thank Mike Talamantes and Kristina Boyanova who I often called when in the darkest moments of PTSD. You helped save my life and I am forever grateful. I'm hoping this book pays your love, friendship, and concern forward to others.

Before writing this book, I had a dilemma, "Which book to write first?" I had several ready to go. My good friend Katie Richards advised me to listen to Jamaican Spiritual teacher Mooji. I found him on YouTube, turned out the lights in my room, lay flat, relaxed on my bed as Katie advised. I hit "play" and Mooji began to talk. Seven minutes into the dialogue I shot out of bed and yelled out to no one in particular, "It's the ER book!" Thank you Mooji for the tools to calm my mind and listen to the universe.

I would like to thank Dr. Patricia Bay for providing amazing perspective and guidance from her 30 years' experience as a counselor for first responders. I appreciate your friendship and guidance.

Introduction

One hundred and eighty-five pages into the manuscript I began to have doubts about the content.

Would the subject matter be too dark?

Would prospective readers be interested in the topic?

I was looking outward. My concern was the consumers, those voracious bookworms who have thousands of titles to choose from every single day.

Why would anyone want to read this book?

So, Forty-One Thousand, Nine Hundred and Forty-Four words into the manuscript I panicked.

Fortunately, my hero dropped by to see how I was doing. This man has held that title and position for forty-seven years. He's my dad.

I saw him and called out, "Hey Pop! Can I talk to you for a minute?"

He smiled, pulled his K-9 trainer ball cap up, scratched his head, and said, "Sure."

We walked out to the gazebo and sat under the fan that was at full blast. I took a deep breath and said, "Am I wasting time writing this book about my experiences in EMS and the ER?"

I paused, looked over at our quaint little pond and continued, "I mean, is this subject matter too dark? Are people even going to want to read this?"

Dad could see I was extremely troubled by the thought that had so rudely invaded my brainwork. Pulling from his invisible book of wisdom that had steered me well these many years, Pop said something very wise, a nugget that immediately put all my frets and fears into perspective, "What's your purpose for writing the book?"

Dad made me look inward.

It was brilliant.

I smiled and replied, "Dad, you could not have asked a better question. Your words just solidified the importance of this book."

Pop smiled and said, "Ok, tell me what you're thinking. What's the purpose of the book?"

Confidently and without hesitation I proclaimed, "First, I want RNs, ER Techs, Medics, EMS, Fire Department and Police to know that they're not alone. There are thousands out there who feel the same. Others with nightmares. Others with a growing darkness that's uncharacteristic for themselves."

Dad smiled, he could see I was getting fired up and excited.

I continued, "Second, I want nurses and medics to read this book and to recommend it or pass along a copy to their administrators, directors, and CEOs and say, 'Boss, I think you should read this.' Conversely, I want employers to take advantage of this rare opportunity to witness the invisible mental and physical strain exerted on the mind and spirit of their employees."

Continuing on I proclaimed, "Third, I want patients and their visiting family members to be aware of some of the behind-the-scenes mini dramas that their nurse and staff is dealing with. I want them to know that their assigned RN is looking at them as an individual case, giving them 100 percent. Yet, also realizing their nurse has four other patients and at that moment she/he may be giving a more critical patient the same 100 percent. Patients and their families need to understand that their nurse knows they or their loved one is not feeling well and she/he understands it's probably one of the worst days of their life."

I was on a roll, the purpose of the book now so evident to me, "Fourth, I want clinicians, psychiatrists and counselors to know that they're on to something great with this Cognitive Processing Therapy program.[1] Psychiatrists and PTSD Counselors need to know that they're helping people and literally saving lives. It works!"

I kept going rapid fire, "Fifth, I want ER, EMS, Fire and Police to know that its ok to get help and talk to someone. They owe it to themselves and their families to do so. The stigma of counseling needs to vanish. For over a decade I never once spoke to a counselor because to do so would have made me look weak to my coworkers. Any utterance of feelings or emotions would bring chides and cries of 'sissy' or other names having to do with female anatomy."

(To you the reader I say the stark truth is that I should have gone to counseling. I should have shaken off that Neanderthal, caveman ideology of manhood. I should have shown respect for myself, my family and sought help. Perhaps my heart and mind would not have become as wounded to the extent that you will soon witness.)

---

[1] CPT is a 12 session psychotherapy for PTSD.

When I finished pouring my heart out to my dad he smiled. He could see I'd had a breakthrough. We hugged, clapped each other on the back.

I said, "Thank you so much Pop! The conversation we just had is going to be the Introduction to the book."

We hugged again and I proclaimed, "Dad, I better get this down while its fresh on my mind."

Straight to my computer, I punched in the letters that became words and then before too long I had the Introduction you see now.

Dear reader, know that reading this book you will get lost in the stories, you're going to feel a wide assortment of emotions. Just know that I am inviting you on this journey with me and I'll take care of you.

So, here we go.

Part One

Molding

Dead Man's Hill

It's always been in me to help people. I was the kid who stood up for the awkward students. If you were crying, I'd ease up to your side, seeing if there was anything I could do to help. Sitting off by yourself, looking sad? Well, I'd pick up my lunchbox and move over to where Little Miss Lonely Heart sat.

I discovered that I had a very strong drive to help in emergencies as well. My very first trauma transport took place in the country of Iceland when I was nine years old. It was winter, 1983, and at least a hundred of us DOD[2] kids were sledding down a massive hill with the ominous name, "Dead Man's Hill."

It seems that hundreds of years before a Viking had died atop the hill and was buried in a cave which had long since been covered over. Well, at least this was the story that Military Brats had been passing on to the next batch of arrivals for decades.

It was bitterly cold on this day, but we kids were bundled up tight with top notch gear. Only hours before I'd been a bit impatient with the many layers of protection

---

[2] Department of Defense. I would normally say Air Force Brats but it was also a Navy base so hence the DOD designation.

22

my mother insisted I wear; snow pants, mittens, woolen cap, coat, insulated boots and scarf.

I complained, "Mom it's gonna be dark before I get out there!"

She laughed, tucked in my scarf, zipped up my coat, checked to be sure my reflectors were visible and released her little Michelin Man out the door.

Reflectors? Yes. It was dark most of the winter. In fact, the longest day was mid-December when the sun would rise at 11am and set between 3 and 4pm. With so much darkness and a multitude of kids outside, the base commander ordered that all children wear reflectors. These contraptions were in the shapes of animals attached to our winter coats.

So, thus attired I headed out the door and immediately saw Catherine Clevenger and Michael Dickerson pulling their sleds heading toward my house. We shouted, laughed, and joined up for the long trek through the snow. Here and there at all points of the compass were smatterings of kids heading to and from the hill, sleds of all shapes, colors, and sizes in tow.

Dead Man's Hill set between two distinct housing areas which were absolutely packed with kids. For, if there's one thing military parents are good at, it's producing offspring. Of course, this was great for us as there were always loads of kids to hang out with.

At the time our housing area was called Tree Housing, and it looked a lot like apartment buildings we have here in the States. There were dozens of four-story buildings inhabited by the families of those who manned Naval Air Station Keflavik.

Next to our housing area was a subdivision of two-story homes that were for the Non-Commissioned Officers. The area was called Birch Housing and was for those with the ranks of Tech Sergeant, Master Sergeant, Chief Petty Officer and so forth. My dad was a Tech Sergeant in the Air Force and a Cop. Because of his rank, and the size of our family, we were slated to move to Birch Housing in a matter of weeks.

Tree Housing and Birch Housing, side by side, meant that Dead Man's Hill was swarmed with kids.

It was a blast!

"Look out!"

"Move it or lose it!"

"Coming through!"

Kids jumped left and right to avoid the human torpedoes slicing through the snow.

A group of us had just zipped down the hill at top speed, trails of snow bursts in our wake. We laughed and awkwardly grabbed the ropes of our sleds as we turned to head back up the towering hill. Snot coursed down our numb rosy cheeked faces. Our winter caps kept sliding down, covering half of our field of vision, and causing us to lift our heads at weirdly jaunted angles. We could have cared less.

Off to our right a kid was trekking up the hill when he suddenly stumbled. As he went to the ground we heard, "Watch out!"

A kid on a sleek fast-moving sled with wooden slats and bright red metal runners was hurtling down the slope at top speed. We turned in time to see this poor stumbling kid look up and take the full force of the sled's momentum right into his mouth.

Wham!

Bodies tumbled end over end, the sled continuing down the hill riderless. There in a heap were the two boys, crying, and holding their heads.

A bunch of us ran over to help. This poor boy had blood gushing out of his face. He was disoriented and unaware how bad off he was until he saw our horrified faces. Then, looking down at the snow that was covered in his own blood he freaked!

His shriek snapped us out of our shock, and we took over the situation. Thoughts of compression to a bleeding wound didn't enter our minds. Our only option, evacuate the casualty!

We threw him down on a sled and took turns dragging our fallen comrade to his home. Sweat poured down rosy cheeks and our lungs heaved for oxygen as we pulled. It was tough work, but there were plenty of kids to help bear the weight.

A couple military brats ran ahead to sound the alarm to this battered soul's mother. I'll never forget the look on her face when she emerged from the door, drying her hands with a dish towel, and seeing her boy's pulverized face for the first time. It was awful.

Reflecting almost forty years I can see that I always had that urge to jump in and help in an emergency.

The fact that, not a year before, I had witnessed my father almost die may have spurred me to action there in Iceland.

That incident took place while we were stateside and living on Lackland Air Force Base in San Antonio, Texas. Dad had been eating a hotdog when he cut a joke, laughed, and promptly inhaled a large chunk of Oscar Meyer's finest down his windpipe.

He did the classic choking pose, both hands wrapped around his throat, with no ability to speak, or breath. I could see the terror in his eyes. Mom initially started to laugh because Dad was always playing jokes on us, but she soon saw the reality.

Our neighbors to the left had a relative visiting. He was often outside smoking a cigarette bragging about being in the medical field.

When my dad began choking, this guy just stood there, paralyzed in fear. I'll never forget it. I was furious at this man, screaming, "Why won't you help my dad!"

I recall flopping down on the sidewalk, beating my fists against the cement, screaming, angry, crying, begging God, the universe, anyone, "Please save my dad!"

Thank God our neighbor to the right was Tech Sergeant Johnson. Hearing my screams he immediately sprang into action. I watched as Sgt. Johnson sprinted toward my home, threw open the screen door and entered. In a matter of minutes Sergeant Johnson was ushering me back into the house. He had performed the Heimlich maneuver on my dad, which instantly ejected the maleficent piece of hot dog across the room.[3]

So, a year later, atop that Viking snow covered Icelandic hill I sprang to action as did my buddies. I would not sit by like that pompous poser who'd not helped my father. I'd be like Tech Sergeant Johnson. I'd be like my dad!

Of course, at that moment in Iceland I had no idea about a future career or even what I hoped the future would hold. Looking back, it all makes perfect sense the way things played out.

---

[3] My father nominated Tech Sgt Johnson for an award and began the proper paper work. It went through channels and months later my father proudly stood by as Tech Sgt. Johnson received an Air Force Commendation Medal.

Smoke Spires

Oklahoma Baptist College
5517 NW 23rd Street
Oklahoma City, OK
April 19, 1995

I was gonna be late to class and it was all the fault of my girlfriend who'd surprised me with homemade peanut butter and Hershey Kiss cookies.

The homemade creations were amazing. Being so enamored with the gift and her smile I'd allowed the time to get away from me. My first clue of my impending tardiness was the startling lack of sound. No students scurrying here and there. Looking at my watch I discovered I had mere seconds until the bell rang so I thanked her again and sprinted down the hall. As I crossed the threshold the bell sounded. I looked at my watch, 9am.

My buddies looked over at me, heckled me a bit but then noticed the plastic container with cookies and changed their tune.

"Don't even think about it," I laughed.

With my briefcase on my lap filling in for a desk, I opened my spiral notebook and prepared to take notes.

It was 9:02.

At that very moment the left wall of our classroom fiercely shook causing the glass in the windows to violently rattle. A millisecond later an invisible wave of pressure coursed over our heads through the rafters causing the ceiling to buckle and moan. Tiny flecks of plaster floated down like snowflakes.

Wham!

The wall on the right side of the room now violently shook making us wonder if the windows would explode.

We just sat there staring at the walls, the ceiling and each other in silence.

Several students sprang to their feet, ran to the windows, and opened the blinds to see if our classroom had been struck by a vehicle off NW 23rd street.

The baffled professor asked, "You guys see anything out there?"

One of my friends exclaimed, "No! I don't see anything out of the ordinary!"

We all wondered what the heck had happened. There was no internet back then, no Wi-Fi for cell phones, in fact, we didn't have cell phones, so we just shrugged our shoulders and continued on with the class.

Emerging out into the hallway I noticed a large gathering of students outside the administration office. Some of the young ladies covered their mouths with their hands. Guys stood quietly shaking their heads.

What could it be?

Stepping up to the window I peered into the office and noticed that a television had been pulled up. There on the TV screen was a large building that looked as if a giant monster had stepped on it. Half of the building was gone, and we could clearly see about seven stories of open internal office spaces.

Loose papers by the thousands floated in the wind amidst large spiraling clouds of billowing black and gray smoke. Dozens of vehicles engulfed in flames surrounded this terrifying spectacle.

Then I heard someone exclaim, "That's downtown!"

Several of us sprinted outside and looked toward the heart of Oklahoma City. There on the horizon were the same spiraling angry black plumes of smoke. This was real.

Back in the hallway I called out, "Hey guys, you can see the smoke from the parking lot!"

Several students ran outside, but I remained by the television transfixed by the horrifying images. Then came the words that would set the course of my next twenty-five years. One of the reporters, live at the scene of carnage, looked into the camera and with a trembling voice pleaded, "We need all medical personnel downtown now! All medical personnel please come downtown now!"

A couple of the students had seen combat in the Persian Gulf during Operation Desert Storm, so they loaded up with a friend who was an RN. Off they went downtown to face the unknown and there I stood with nothing to give. My country, my city was in need, and I had nothing to contribute. Deep within me was a great revulsion to this fact.

Right then and there, staring at the horrific images on the screen, taking in the holocaust that Timothy McVeigh had created I made a decision. Never again would I have nothing to offer my community in an emergency. I would never stand idly by while others suffered.

I soon took a course at OSU's city campus[4], Emergency Medical Technician, EMT. That was for me. The images of medics running toward danger, death and destruction had seared into my brain. That was me. I was going to help.[5]

Thus began my career in Emergency Medicine.

On a quiet day that was shattered by violence Timothy McVeigh had snuffed out 168 precious lives and wounded many more. His act of violence that was meant to demoralize a nation spurred me to action. For the next twenty-five years I would be instrumental in saving thousands of lives. In addition, I would teach dozens and dozens of medics, nurses, interns, resident doctors, and others who would likewise go on to save lives.

In a way, that shock wave of April 19, 1995, continues to go on and on as more and more lives are saved by those I helped to save and those I've trained to do the same.

---

[4] I took the course with my sister Marnie who turned out to be an awesome medic. Our instructors were firemen who had been at the Murrah building rescuing those who survived. Their stories made our training all the more serious.

[5] Only years later would I realize I'd become my hero Mister Rogers's own mother's words when she spoke of times when bad things happen, "Look for the helpers. You will always find people who are helping."

Nothings Gonna Happen

Canadian County, Oklahoma

Before there was saving of people there was the important fact that I needed to be trained. Part of that training, and my favorite part, were the required ride outs we had to do with local Ambulance Agencies.

All EMT students are required to participate and successfully complete at least 60 hours of "clinical hours". These hours are to be divided between Ambulance ride outs and shadowing someone at a local Emergency Room.

This was a huge test for me for it's one thing to have book knowledge and quite another to have the knowledge of the streets. As I prepared for my first ride on an ambulance, I brought a little flip chart that fits into a pant cargo pocket. I had pens, a stethoscope and a brand-new uniform that was pressed.

I had the knowledge, but would I be able to use it during an actual emergency. It's one thing to perform well in a classroom setting with the stakes quite low, and another when the stakes are life and death. This is a fear that we students faced. Would we measure up?

One guy comes to mind. This EMT student scored a 100% on every test, quiz and then with the bonus points was always bumped up to 105. The dude had a photographic memory and just flat out excelled. During the practice sessions he flourished as the protocols just popped into his brain. However, during his ride outs with the ambulance crew he froze on every call he went on. He was unable to process the information. He was paralyzed by fear.

In later years, when I was training nursing students or EMT students in the ER I'd think back on that guy and I'd tell my students, "The real test will be when an emergency comes in through the door. Will you be able to perform? When the adrenaline flows, and fear drenched anxiety starts to well up in your chest will you be able to access the files in your brain that your training has provided? Only time will tell."

The students would swallow hard and stare at their feet. I continued, "Look, we're all afraid and nervous. I mean, let's get real, someone's dying. My hand still shakes with adrenaline. The difference is shown in those who use that fear to make them sharper, calmer. Take a breath and fall back on your training."

During a code[6] I'd force myself to deliberately talk slow, precise, and clear. I knew from my voracious appetite in World War II history books that fear is contagious. If you sound rattled those around, may start to falter.

During one code I sidled up next to a nurse, leaned in close and whispered, "You're the only one yelling here. Stay calm, you got this."

But, I'm getting ahead of myself. Let's back up a bit.

Back in 1997 in Oklahoma City I was terrified and unsure if I would have what it took to perform.

How would I perform during an emergency?

My first ride out was with Mercy Ambulance Service that serviced the Bethany, Warr Acres areas around Oklahoma City. I really enjoyed working with these crews because their ambulances were new and had all the latest bells and whistles, literally.

---

[6] A "Code" is what we would call a patient who had lost vital signs or was beginning to show the symptoms of vital signs that were becoming unstable. Examples would be someone we had to intubate or someone we did COPR on.

I soon learned that there's a common superstition among EMS, Fire, Police and ER, "If you have a student or an observer, nothing is going to happen."

It seemed to be true of my first shift. The hours ticked by with not a single call. I was getting bummed out. Would all my ambulance hours be superficially earned?

Now this may sound strange or even insensitive but let me explain this eagerness for a call in a different way.

A saying that all of the Emergency Services lived by was, "We don't want bad things to happen to people, but in this life such things will happen and when they do we want to be the ones to take care of you."

I wanted to help. My desire to test myself and see if I had what it takes was incredibly strong. I was impatient but it mattered little as hour after hour went by with no action.

Then finally it came. The call.

In the wee hours of the morning, around 2am the little 2"x 3" black pagers[7] affixed to the belts of the paramedics

---

[7] This was a stone-age piece of technology that beeped when someone needed to talk to us. It showed the number of the person paging us, which then

began to chirp. The neon green screen of the pager illuminated revealing the call we were being dispatched to. It was a roll-over accident on I-40 just east of Warr Acres. This was going to be remote.

The lights were switched on and the siren began to wail as we flew down the highway toward the unknown. I was pumped!

As the ambulance raced to the scene so did my heart. I was nervous, terrified, and excited. I was finally doing it, on my way to my first scene.

As we pulled up to the scene one of the paramedics lifted a radio and reported that we'd arrived. I pulled on some medical gloves, donned my reflective vest, and grabbed the trauma bag.

Stepping out into the night I was immediately struck by how cold and damp the country air felt. It seemed to penetrate my bones. My teeth chattered. Was this nerves? The cold air? Or perhaps a combination of the two?

My steps provoked angry grinding sounds from shattered glass. Off to the right the bushes and trees

---

required us to find a phone with which to return the call. Ours were a little fancier because they actually showed a text message regarding our call.

seemed to dance with the staccato blue and red strobes. Blue, Blue, Blue, Red, Red, Red, Blue, Blue, Red, Red, and so on.

My senses were elevated so I was taking it all in.

Ahead I could see a couple Sherriff Deputies and a State Trooper had shut down one of the lanes with flares and were using flashlights to move the occasional vehicle safely along.

A fire truck was soon joined by another and in an instant, I could hear the sound of a generator come to life. In a matter of seconds, the exhaust joined the already complex mixture of aromas that seared their odor into my memory; diesel saturated grass, decaying woodlands, upturned earth, the slight smell of fog, the soot permeated coats of firemen and now the stench of exhaust from the generator.

Within seconds after the generator was kicked on several banks of lights clicked on punching broad paths of light through the trees revealing a pickup truck in a serious predicament.

It seems the driver had lost control and rolled up hill smashing trees to splinters. When the momentum was lost, unforgiving gravity took over causing the truck to then roll back down the hill. Unfortunately, the driver was tossed from the vehicle on the last of its rolls, and as the truck came to rest on its roof the driver's left leg was pinned underneath.

There were some serious dangers still present to both the driver and EMS.

The truck had not come all the way back down the hill because it was resting against a tree that creaked under the pressure. We were still on the hill so this meant that if the tree gave way, the truck would continue down the hill. In addition, diesel fuel had spilled out and saturated the grass all around and it had thoroughly soaked our pants as we kneeled in the grass to render aid.[8]

Firemen had run water hoses up the hill to our location and had saturated the grass around us to disperse the concentrated fuel. In addition, they stood by, ready to hose us all down should a spark ignite the fumes.

The fire captain, who oversaw the scene, would not authorize us to enter the vehicle or tend to the patient until the upside-down truck had been secured. No need for further casualties.

---

[8] Even today, all these years later, the smell of diesel fuel takes me to this moment.

We used this time to talk to the patient and triage his injuries by asking the obvious question, "Where are you hurting?"

He of course complained about his leg and a bump on his head. Our flashlights revealed that he did in fact have a scalp laceration which was oozing blood, but it did not appear to be life threatening. The trapped leg was an unknown. The paramedic explained the safety situation to the driver who took the news in stride.

I watched two groups of firefighters take chains and attach them to the axle of the upside-down truck. These chains were gingerly worked around the metal and then secured to large sturdy and undamaged trees further up the hill. In this way the truck would not roll on top of us as we worked to free this unfortunate guy.

Within minutes the scene was secured by the fire department, and we were given permission to tend to our patient and work with the firemen on the best way to extract him.

The awkward angle was wreaking havoc on his joints. A huge concern of ours was that the weight of the truck might have interrupted the flow of blood to his foot. We needed to move quickly. Yet safely.

As I stood there, I noted that the position of the roof of the cab and the leg meant that the foot must be... right there! I had an idea, which I voiced to my preceptor, "Why not dig the dirt out from around the upside-down cab. Since we can't get down to the foot why not come up from underneath it."

"Great idea! Get to it!" was the paramedics reply.

I went down to all fours and crawled under the truck. As it was resting at an odd angle there was a bit of a void I could use to get close. The Fire Department Captain saw what I was up to, positioned a light to shine in the space and exclaimed, "Excellent idea! You keep digging and I'll move the dirt out of your way."

I was digging with my shears to some effect but one of the firemen provided a pick and I used that to scrape away at the grass and dirt. In a matter of a few minutes, I could see the sole of his tennis shoe.

I called out, "Hey! I can see his shoe!"

One of the paramedics crawled underneath, reached up with his shears, cut off the shoestrings, and then cut the shoe from around the foot.

He felt for a pulse and called out, "I've got a strong pulse here."

With a few more minutes of diligent digging, we were able to tunnel all the way to the point where the edge of the truck pinned his leg against the earth. A few more digs and then a shout of joy went up! Our patient was free of the vehicle.

A cervical collar had already been placed on his neck by the other paramedic. As such, we placed the rigid backboard on the ground beside our guy and secured him to it with multiple straps.

Four fire fighters gathered around the backboard with the paramedics and I heard one say, "On the count of three, lift straight up and head down the hill to our stretcher."

Meanwhile I was gathering up the equipment we had used under the truck. As I stepped out from under the vehicle the Fire Department Captain smacked me on the shoulder and gruffly said, "Good job!"

My heart swelled with pride, for a young man worth his salt craves the approval of older and wiser men. I'll never forget that moment, but such luxurious thoughts were for the future. I moved quickly down the hill for we had to assess our patient in detail and determine the injuries he'd sustained.

I made notes in my EMT book as the Initial Assessment was performed. It was intriguing to watch the paramedic expertly assess his patient. All the notes that the paramedic jotted down would be used to brief the Emergency Room staff once we arrived.

Our patient was indeed hurting but he was stable. As we walked through the Ambulance Bay doors a nurse pointed to the room assigned to our patient. As I passed by I noticed a curious look on the face of the RN. She stared at me but said nothing.

"What's her problem?" I thought.

In the trauma room the paramedic described the scene and injuries. The report was delivered in an expert manner and only took seconds to give. As he spoke the ER staff worked as a team removing clothing and inspecting every inch of this poor guy.

Within a few minutes we were walking down the hall feeling good about the amazing job we'd done.

A nurse passing by smiled and laughed as she asked, "Have you seen yourself in the mirror?"

I nervously laughed, "No, why?"

She giggled and said, "Well, there's a restroom over there. Go take a look."

My reflection revealed a mud caked EMT student who was so focused on the job that he'd failed to reckon on his appearance. My face was smeared with Canadian County dried rust-colored mud, and my blue pants and shirt were now a disgraceful display of muddy splashes.

I laughed and realized that the paramedics had of course seen my despicable appearance but chose not to say a word. It was a good prank and one that brought many laughs. I didn't mind for I knew the guys were proud of how I'd performed and that was all that mattered to me.

Within an hour we were back at the station, the vehicle was cleaned, and we were all officially off shift.

I packed up my backpack, slung it over my shoulder and headed out the door. Walking toward my vehicle I heard a voice call out, "Hey Dennis!"

I turned and saw it was one of my paramedic preceptors.

Before I could say a word, he called out, "You did good tonight. When you start looking for a job give me a call."

"Thanks!" I replied, "I sure will."

A grin as wide as the Mississippi crossed my face. Someone I respected had seen my worth.

On this night I learned that I did indeed have "It." I ran toward danger, hungered to be involved and problem solved at every opportunity. My first day had not been a bust for I'd gained intimate details about myself and though the mirror reflected a mud caked figure, it also revealed an EMT in the making.

My molding had begun.

Taxi Service

With the passing of examinations, I was awarded my certificate of completion of the Oklahoma State University EMT course. Within months I was back home in San Antonio to stay and ready to take the Texas EMT Certification Test.

It was a breeze and I passed with flying colors.

Now, to find a place to put these skills to use.

Looking through the yellow pages I found the address of a company called Medic One Ambulance. I liked the name, so I decided to try them first. I'd show up in a suit and tie like I'd been raised to do.

Having gone to Bible College right out of high school I was incredibly disciplined. I had to wear a shirt and tie each day to class. Most times I just wore a suit coat as well because the classrooms were always so cold. So, this dressing up was really just par for the course for me.

This well-orchestrated "dressing for something important" ritual went something like this.

First on was my crisp stark white t-shirt. Then came my dress pants that I'd embellished with a tight crease down the front of each leg. I then donned my ironed starched white collared shirt. Once this article was buttoned up and secured, I looped my tie around my neck in a Half Windsor.[9]

Then came the black socks to match my black belt. It was then time for my black shoes which I'd expertly shined the night before.

A splash of Old Spice and I reached over and grabbed my suit coat which would stay on a hanger until I arrived at my destination across town.

Thirty-five minutes later, pulling onto Franklin Street from Austin Highway my destination was immediately on the left. Unimpressive building to say the least.

Faded lime green brick walls were covered by a giant roof of rusted metal sheeting. The business complex was configured so that the office entrances all faced away from the road, so I was essentially looking at the rear of the building.

---

[9] Also known as the single Windsor knot, it is a way of tying a necktie which produces a neat, triangular knot.

Looking down the long row of guacamole colored brick I could see six window mounted A/C units trying desperately to comfort those occupying the spaces within.

I raised my eyebrows and thought, "Well, this should be interesting."

The gate to the barbed wire topped fence was open so I pulled through and parked. I then noticed a sleek ambulance with the words "Medic One" stenciled on the side. It was the same type of modern snub-nosed box unit I had trained on in Bethany, Oklahoma so I was excited.

Stepping through the office door I was greeted by the owner of the company, a tall, lanky, gregarious fella named Thomas France.[10] Mr. France had a huge smile and was very welcoming. The office personnel could not believe how sharp I looked. They never imagined someone showing up for an interview dressed in that fashion.

In a matter of minutes, I had the job and was presented two new light blue uniform shirts that would soon sport both my Texas EMT patch and Medic One Ambulance patch. I was officially on an ambulance crew.

---

[10] This is a pseudonym. I was never able to track him down again. He was a tremendous guy. I hope he reads this book one day and knows how much I esteem him and appreciate his many kindnesses to me.

Ambulance crews typically rotate a lot due to scheduling changes but I'm the type of guy who can work with anyone. My paramedic partners were always great guys but of course very different in their personalities.

I was once partnered with a paramedic who was a quiet family man who did nothing but the bare minimum. He was not lazy, per se, just efficient. I know it sounds like I'm being generous with my description but that's the way he worked. He'd been doing the job a long time and had no ego about what he did so he was not concerned with image. He looked professional but there were no frills to his work and indeed none to his personality. He was just, well, there.

Another partner I had sported a very fashionable mullet that was well groomed and would've made Andre Agassi[11] jealous. This guy was always on the prowl for women, but his preference baffled me. He liked the toothless, gravelly voiced barflies who smoked and cussed as much as he did.

Not my style but to each his own.

These characters were quite different than I was, but I learned from them. They taught me to see through the fog

---

[11] A tennis star of the early 1990s.

of noise and smells. They helped me get my nerves in check.

Unfortunately, the job was incredibly mind numbing.

The reality of working at Medic One was that most of the calls we were dispatched to were transfers from nursing homes to clinics. These were not emergencies, just expensively glorified taxi service calls.

We'd pull up to a nursing home whose sign inevitably contained the words "Oaks", "Manor", "Village" or "Heights." The lofty name was never as high as the ammonia odor wafting through the corridors. We tried to hold our breath as we walked the dank dismal halls listening to the cries for assistance, the moans of pain and the delirious ramblings of those hopelessly lost in their own minds.

Here and there at odd angles in the halls poor souls sat awkwardly in wheelchairs that had long since lost their shine. Vacant stares. Streams of drool. The fruitless lunges on legs devoid of strength. I couldn't wait to get out of there.

Day after day it's what I did, drive people to their appointments. It was incredibly unfulfilling and a long way from the Emergency aspect I'd signed up for, but I gained experience and that was priceless.

A Woman Scorned

Near my home was a Volunteer Fire Department and one day I stopped in to see what I had to do to become a member. Turns out the process was relatively easy. I filled out a bunch of Documents and attended the county fire academy.

We had a department that hungered for training. We'd take the trucks out, hook up to a hydrant and practice attacking a fire. We attended classes at other county departments learning new techniques and keeping our skills and equipment squared away. It was a blast.

One of the perks of my EMT license was that I was authorized to respond directly to medical calls from my home. I was given oxygen tanks, airway bags and a trauma bag. On my hip I wore a black pager that would only go off if our department had a call. A siren was hooked up to my vehicle and a magnetic red strobe light was placed in the back seat. Should I get a call I would plug it in to the cigarette lighter, feed the cord through the window and slap that baby on the roof. The sound of the light bar's giant magnet grabbing the roof of my car always made me smile. I was a full-fledged, genuine woo-woo.

One night, while watching a TV show my pager screeched its piercing call to stations, scaring the crap out of me. The tone was an extremely high-pitched chirp followed by our identifying tones which were likewise an incredibly high tone followed by a mid-ranged one.

I leapt out of the recliner and slid on my EMT pants and Fire Dept shirt. As I dressed, I could hear Dispatch say, "Northwest respond to a shooting at…"

I grabbed my radio and sprinted to my vehicle. The address given was less than three minutes from my home.

With my red strobe light engaged I pulled out into the street but kept the siren off, so I'd not disturb the neighborhood. I mean, no one was out at that hour anyway.

Heading to the scene I asked Dispatch, "Fire Alarm, this is Medic One. Is S.O. on the scene?"

Within a second the answer crackled across my handheld, "Northwest Medic One[12], be advised Sheriff's Office is on scene and reports it is secure."

---

[12] It was a coincidence that my call sign was "Medic One" and that I also worked for the EMS company, Medic One.

"Copy that dispatch. Medic One out," was my confident sounding sign-off. Well, at least I hoped I sounded confident.

Pulling up to the scene I could see three Sheriff patrol cars were already there. In fact, I was surprised to see that yellow tape restricted access to the entire front of the home.

I grabbed my radio and notified Fire Alarm[13] that I'd arrived on scene. Then I picked up my trauma bag and made my way toward the tape barrier.

I couldn't help but be reminded of the multiple Documentaries I'd scene with tape just like this. This time though I was the one walking toward it and just like the movies a deputy lifted it up so I could pass underneath. I thanked him and heard him mutter, "You won't be needing any of that gear."

I smiled and nervously wondered what he meant. The hard creases in the Deputies face told a tale of years of experience. Was he jaded or just ribbing me? I walked on and then through the front door which was wide open.

---

[13] Our dispatch service.

The home was very clean but remarkably unlit. The only light came from two lamps in the living room between which emanated the sound of whimpering.

Seated on the couch was a middle-aged woman wearing shorts and a t-shirt. Her elbows rested on her thighs and her hands covered her face. Tears coursed down her hands and smacked the tops of her thighs as her shoulders jolted and heaved with emotion. My gaze rose from this lady to the Deputy who was jotting down notes in a small yellow steno pad.

The Deputy cocked his head over his left shoulder in a jerking motion, which I rightfully took to indicate the person I was there for was in one of the back rooms of the house.

From one of the rear bedrooms I could hear chatter on a radio. I figured this must be where the third Deputy was located.

Suddenly the radio on my hip squelched and a crackling voice belched out, "Dispatch this is Northwest Fire Engine 2 en route."

I knew my back-up was at least eight minutes away. A long time in this setting.

My radio traffic caught the attention of the third Deputy who poked his head out of a side bedroom and motioned me to proceed down the long dark hallway.

As I walked down the corridor, I could sense the family portraits on the walls on each side of me. Faces staring. Mute.

Entering the room, I was immediately struck by an incredibly overpowering odor of iron. Yes iron, but there was also something different that hung like a cold, wet towel over my head. I'd never felt, smelt, or sensed this strange atmosphere before this moment. There was a strong musty stench that worked through the iron.

What could it be?

There, on the bed fully naked, was a man lying comfortably with his head resting on a fluffy pillow that was encased in tan silk material. Clean sheets were pulled down past the man's ankles. The bed itself, a scene of tranquility.

The rest of the room was in shambles. Dresser drawers were torn out. Clothing littered the floor. Pictures hung at odd angles and a couple lamps were smashed and strewn about.

Stepping over the items on the floor I made my way around to the other side of the bed. There I noticed the reason for the aroma of iron. The left side of the man's face was gone. Actually, I found it splattered up against the wall. Bits of flesh, brain and bone were even then slowly sliding down the wall to the floor trim.

Next to the bed on the floor was a large chrome colored handgun that could more accurately be described as a hand cannon. It looked to be one of those "Dirty Harry" .357 magnums.

The lady on the couch was now hysterical, "He was always hitting me! I had enough!"

Yeah, she sure did. When he got drunk and passed out after a long night of chasing her around the house, and working her over, he fell asleep. While this guy slept in his alcohol induced coma, she retrieved the gigantic handgun from its special place and crept up to the bed. The only sound was his obnoxious snoring and the metallic click as the hammer was pulled back on the handgun.

Wham!

The explosion of gunpowder in the small, confined space left the battered woman momentarily deaf. The dude was dead before the bullet exited his brain.

I checked a pulse, but it was merely a formality as there was brain tissue all over the wall and bed spread. The dude was a goner. The ambulance soon arrived and one of the paramedics officially declared the guy deceased. I now stood in an active murder scene. Time for me to get out with as little impact as possible on my surroundings.

I'll never forget the smell of iron and the large pool of coagulated blood that jiggled like Jell-O anytime the bed was bumped. The sights and the smells will last a lifetime. It was my first acquaintance with murder and would not be my last. I can tell you that it was not company I favored.

Last Door on the Right

You know it may seem crazy but the one constant that I always enjoyed about working with the Fire Department was that nothing was constant.

Would there be a shift with a dozen calls or a shift with none? The calls we received, would they be all medical, all trauma or a combination of the two? Of the trauma calls would they be predominantly all falls, or would they be a mixture of falls, motor accidents, assaults, or mishaps? Of the multiple variations how many of these would be adult and how many pediatric?

If it was an assault, or a domestic abuse case well then emotions would be running high, and safety would be a necessity but not guaranteed. The Sheriff deputies did their best, but they couldn't be everywhere at once.

Then add to the mix the unknowns regarding the setting.

Will there be family pets that will tear into us? Who will check on the dogs after we leave to feed them and be sure they get water?

Are we heading to a trailer, a vehicle, a home, a place of business or the outdoors? If it's a home or trailer what would be the condition of the dwelling? Would there be mounds of trash overrun with vermin or would it be a pristine environment? Would the patient be sitting in a chair or wedged between the toilet and the bathtub? When we leave with the patient is the oven off? Is the patient's personal oxygen tank turned off, so they don't return home to an empty tank and thus another medical emergency?

Will they speak English, or would I have to do my best with the Spanish I'd picked up? What if they spoke a language no one knew? How would I figure out what was going on?

Sprinkle into that mix the vortex of human personalities that swirl around us every day. Would the family be condescending, irritable, hysterical, concerned, or aloof? Would the family be helpful or a hindrance?

Such is a glimpse into the complexities of responding to those who've called 911.

How about an example.

One night I was lying in bed sleeping soundly when my pager shrieked its piercing call. I sprang out of bed and geared up.

"Northwest Respond to a Shortness of Breath at…"

I picked up my radio and pressed the transmit button, "Dispatch this is Northwest Medic One, show me en route at this time."

Within minutes I pulled up to the house and was struck by the serenity of the suburban street. There was not a sound to be heard, not even the far-off siren of my backup. Quite alone I grabbed my equipment, reported to dispatch that I was on scene and stepped toward the home.

Wait, was this the correct address?

The house was completely blacked out. No porch lights. No warm glow peeking through pulled curtains. No garage lights bordering the driveway. Even the county streetlamp had failed in its nightly duty to illuminate the scene.

Nothing. Just complete darkness.

Pulling out my flashlight I shone it on the house and found the address placard. I pressed the transmit button, "Dispatch, this is Medic One, what was that address for this medical?"

Within a second the address was relayed to me. Sure enough, I was at the correct location.

I knocked on the door and stood patiently waiting for a response. There was none. Seconds ticked by.

Would we have to break into this home? My mind wandered and I imagined an elderly woman, collapsed on a bathroom floor with a broken hip, unable to move.

I tried again but this time I pounded hard and called out, "Northwest Fire Department! Anyone home?! Did you call 911?!?"

Minutes had gone by and still no response. I went to a tactical channel on my radio and let our responding fire crew know that we may have a situation requiring a forced entry into the home, and as such we may need the Sheriff Department on scene.

A few seconds later the door slowly opened and revealed a house completely illuminated. I mean, it seemed every light was on in the house. They had some incredible black out curtains let me tell you.

I shook my head in disbelief and with a hint of frustration asked, "Did you call 911?"

The guy looks me up and down as if he's trying to comprehend why on earth I'd be there. As he's contemplating his words, I can't help but notice that my red strobe lights are bouncing beams off this dude's shiny forehead. I also noted a person sitting awkwardly erect on a couch in the living room. Meanwhile a movie played on a large TV screen.

Surreal!

The zombie standing before me says nothing but turns to let me pass. As I step through the threshold, I notice that there's a third adult quite busy washing dishes. I reflected on all the minutes I stood on the doorstep waiting for someone to answer the door.

I was a bit irritated when I asked, "Did you guys call 911 or what?"

No one said a word.

Then, suddenly as if snapped out of a trance, the woman washing dishes flatly responds, "Yeah."

Her single word hung in the air for an eternity.

I finally asked the question I thought was obvious but apparently not, "Ok, where's the patient?"

The haggard lady points toward a hallway and mumbles, "Last door on the right."

It was about this time my radio went off and I heard my station report they were en route with a crew of three. It made me feel a little safer knowing backup was coming because these folks were giving me the willies.

Stepping quickly down the hall I turned into the last room on the right and noticed a very large naked woman lying on a bed, flat on her back.

I entered and called out, "Hello! Northwest Fire Department how are you? What's going on?"

The ladies' eyes were wide open, and she uttered not a word.

Well, this was quite the talkative family!

I reached down and touched her arm with my gloved hand. As I did, I called out loudly, "Hello ma'am how are you doing?"

She didn't answer and her skin was ice cold. Oh crap!

I vigorously shook her and when I did, she let out a long slow trail of air from her mouth that sounded a lot like an exhale. I reached for her neck…no pulse.

CRUD!

I attempted to get on the bed and start CPR but when I knelt on the bed I fell sideways across her naked body. It was a friggin waterbed!

The water level was way too low, so I was bobbing and weaving all over the place. Each time I righted myself and attempted to do a compression I'd lose my balance. I tried a couple more chest compressions, but it was impossible. Each time I attempted to thrust down she just simply melted into the bed.

Oh crap, crap! I must get her off this freaking ocean!

I pull and pull but she doesn't budge an inch. The water is dispersing around her creating a wall that I can't bring her through. This is a nightmare. Sweat pours from my forehead, streaks down my nose and drips onto her bare discolored chest.

I tried rolling her on her side and this did the trick. Problem was I had to completely roll her which I can assure you was far from graceful and most assuredly not contained in any manual.

Well, with her body finally propped on the edge I braced my knee against her back and tried to guide her to the floor as gently as I could.

Yeah right.

Thump!

She was on the ground. It wasn't graceful but she was down.

At this moment a male family member poked his head in and asks, "How's it going in here?"

The words that instantly came to mind thankfully got stuck before crossing my lips. I managed to say, "Not good."

First thing was to give her a couple minutes of chest compressions which I did with no problem now that she was on a hard surface. With a good run of compressions completed I moved to her airway.

Opening her mouth, I was greeted with a sight I'd not imagined. Her mouth was chuck full of bananas. I mean, absolutely stuffed with the gooey substance.

I opened my airway bag and removed my suction equipment. First though I did something your trained not to, I placed a plastic airway adjunct between her teeth and then stuck my finger down into her throat and scooped out as much gooey mush as I could get.[14] I then suctioned out the rest and was gratified to hear a swoosh of air enter her lungs. I had a patent airway!

I gave her a couple of good breaths from my Ambu Bag[15] and then switched back over to chest compressions. I was sweating profusely, and I could only watch as sweat dripped from my nose and onto this poor lady's face. I tried swiping my shoulders across my own face hoping to sponge the sweat, but it had little effect. I had to continue.

After another round of compressions and puffs of air I saw black boots in my periphery. I looked up and there stood two San Antonio Fire Department Paramedics. The ambulance crew had arrived!

The one closest to me spoke up, "Whatcha got?"

---

[14] We were trained to never put your fingers past the line of a patient's teeth for the obvious reason that they might spasm, seize and bite down taking your fingers off.

[15] A hard plastic hollow contraption that is connected to oxygen. When you push down on the bag it forces air into a mask that covers the patient's mouth, thus forcing air into their lungs. This replaced the need for "mouth to mouth".

As he finished the word "got" he let go of a glove he was putting on causing it to snap against his wrist making the familiar popping sound.

I was exhausted but I continued pumping away.

I looked up at him and said, "I got nothing. No pulse."

The second paramedic said, "Let's drag her out into the living room so we can have more room to work."

Easier said than done. She was way too heavy for us to carry through the narrow doorway and then down the tight hall to the living room. So, that left us with a single option, we took her arms and drug her.

Over the carpet she had walked many a time went her cold naked body. Passed the photos of her children and grandchildren smiling brightly went this lady who deserved more respect than we could provide. My gut ached as we walked.

In a matter of seconds we were in the carpeted dining room and the two paramedics began to work her. They relieved me of CPR since I'd been doing it on my own for quite a while.

As one paramedic did chest compressions the other started an IV. Meanwhile I squeezed the Ambu Bag pushing oxygen into her lungs.

Epi was administered once and then again, a couple minutes later. The monitor was hooked up to her but when the paramedic stopped compressing on her chest to check for a pulse, there was none there and no electrical activity on the monitor.[16]

By this time our fire department guys arrived and brought in the stretcher from San Antonio's ambulance. We loaded her up and they were off to the hospital.[17]

The fellas were patting me on the back, "Good job Blocker!"

Someone threw me a towel to wipe the sweat off my face. Soon a bottle of water was thrust in my hands, and I was swigging it down.

Strange but it didn't feel like a good job. I knew I'd done my best, but I also knew that there was something odd about the response of that family.

---

[16] The famous "flat line" you see in movies or TV shows.
[17] She did not survive.

For example, why had they taken so long to answer the door? Why did they not immediately usher me to the bedroom? Why were they not there to assist me in placing her on the floor? So many questions!

The incident is one I obviously never forgot and there are several reasons.

One, the aloof attitude of the family who, while they watched TV and washed the dishes, their family member died.

Second, why was the bedroom door wide open and the lights all on in her room?

Three, why was she naked, flat on her back on a waterbed with a mouth full of bananas?

Four, why was her family so uninterested in what was happening?

Five, who called 911 and how long did they wait before they called?

Six, why had they taken so long to answer the door?

Seven, why did not the guy who answered the door take me direct to the patient?

This call was a huge eyeopener for me and taught me early on not to take anything for granted when responding to a call. A "Shortness of Breath" can quickly turn into something quite unforgettable.

A Bridge, a Seat, and a Dilemma

One long and cold night, after a couple hours of rigorous training at the fire station, we were busy loading up our hoses, wiping down the trucks and stowing our gear when we heard our neighboring fire district get a call for a major accident.

We knew this particular department depended on us for mutual aid, so we prepped our gear and made sure everything was topped off, just in case we were needed.

We sat around the radio in a fashion reminiscent of old photos of long ago. A time when families gathered around their radios listening to the latest crime drama serial.

A calm, clear voice emanated from the speaker attached to our wall beside the calendar, "Dispatch, be advised we have multiple injured patients on scene. Please advise AirLife that we will need them. Stand by for our location."

An equally cool and calm voice replied, "Copy that, AirLife will be notified."

With that our chief told us, "We're going to stage close to the scene. I have a gut feeling they're going to need us."

Crews were assigned to each truck and then the Chief looked at me and said, "Dennis, grab the trauma bag. You're with me."

Off we went to stage near their district. Now, we'd not officially been asked for, so we could not proceed with our lights and sirens, but we made good time anyway. Our ears were glued to the speakers, and we could tell that the department was stretched for help.

Then came the call, "Dispatch, can you please request our mutual aid respond to our location. We're gonna require more manpower."

We arrived within minutes because our Chief had tremendous foresight. Parking near the scene of carnage we donned our bunker gear,[18] affixed our hard hats and made way to the scene on foot.

There was debris everywhere.

The scene of the catastrophic crash originated at the top of a bridge that crossed a small dried-up stream. A teenaged driver, behind the wheel of his pickup truck, had been driving extremely fast hoping to do a Dukes of Hazard leap at the crest of the bridge.

---

[18] The heavy jacket, pants, boots and gloves that firemen wear.

His attempt to go airborne was successful but the impact of his tires with the asphalt caused his vehicle to spin in a circle. He was out of control and halfway around a second circle when he began skidding backwards and plowed into an oncoming minivan.

Walking up the bridge I could see that one helicopter had already landed. The side door was open, and the flight crew were loading a patient.

One of the firemen, who'd been on scene since the beginning, saw my gaze locked onto the helicopter and called out, "We found that guy unconscious in the bed of the pickup. The truck was sliding backwards when it hit the minivan. That poor guy went right through the back window of that truck. Crazy ain't it?"

All I could manage was an inadequate, "Yeah, that's crazy all right."

Taking a few more steps I could hear the deep base whomp, whomp, whomp of another approaching rescue helicopter. This one was a Huey, painted white with a red cardiac rhythm stenciled on the side. It soon made the scene and landed on the other side of the bridge amidst a broiling cloud of dust, dirt, and decaying brush. Firemen with their visors down and their flashlights up expertly guided the large bird down.

Our Chief had been asked to manage the scene involving the minivan as the other Fire Chief was busy at the pickup truck. Approaching the van, I could hear the pitiful grunting and moans of the driver who was in immense pain that seemed to rack his body in waves. The driver's face was obscured by gore matted hair and wide rivulets of blood.

The front compartment of the minivan bore stark testament to the forces involved. The entire engine block was pushed into the driver's compartment snaping both of this poor guy's femurs.

Standing at the rear of the minivan the Chief said something, but truth be told I was unclear what he said. It sounded a lot like, "Put me through this window." So, I hefted him up and put him through the back window which was smashed out.

Once inside, he laughed and said, "Well, I guess I'm going in the van."

I laughed, "Sorry Chief, I thought you asked me to help you get in there."

As I spoke the Chief began passing me various tools and equipment from the back of the minivan which obviously belonged to a handyman. Tools of all sorts came my way as well as hoses and appliances. One by one they were passed through the window and a path was cleared toward the driver.

So, why go through the back window?

Well, the doors on both sides of the minivan were buckled and could not be budged. There was no better way to get to this guy than through the back. Not to mention the fact that the dash was officially in the passenger seat. Space was at a premium.

Meanwhile, Chief was finally up to the driver and because he was inside, he had more access to his injuries. The patient was assessed from head to toe, and honestly the outcome looked grim.

"Dennis, I need you in here!" shouted my Chief.

The words shot out the back window and within seconds I was crawling in with a trauma bag.

Ahead of me I could hear the driver mumbling something to my Chief who was doing his best to reassure this bloody human pulp.

Firefighters outside the vehicle were unfolding a blanket that was going to be placed over the driver. Its purpose was to shield him from errant shards of metal and glass once the "Jaws" started ripping the vehicle to pieces.

Meanwhile I was passing bandages and 4x4 dressings to my Chief who was doing a most impressive head to toe physical assessment stopping only to plug lacerations and stemming the loss of life sustaining blood.

By this time the engine in our faces had begun to smoke. While fire fighters worked their prybars trying to pop the hood, my Chief yelled out to no one in particular, "Hey! Make sure you guys have a two-inch attack line[19] charged and ready to go in case this van goes up in flames!"

Now, I of course knew this was a possibility but something about hearing those words solidified the situation we were in. We never wavered though. We were with our patient through whatever might come.

Of course, we weren't looking to be heroes, but there was just no way we were going to leave this guy unless we were ordered out.

---

[19] A fire hose that is hooked up to a fire truck or fire hydrant, primed and ready to dispense water.

A minute later, off to my right, I caught movement and could see a couple firefighters standing, one in front of the other, both holding the requested attack line. Beads of life preserving water slowly oozed through the nozzle and dripped to the ground, heralding its presence, and calming my nerves.

During this time there was an intense debate between my Chief and those outside the vehicle. The noise of the generators, the fire trucks and the idling helicopter meant that conversations were shouted. It appeared those involved were in a heated argument, but such was not the case.

The focus of the debate; to cut the steering wheel or leave it in place.

The darn thing was practically mashed into our patient's chest, so it was a huge hindrance to the evaluation of his chest injuries and breathing.

The more significant problem was that the airbag had not deployed on impact. The steering wheel was literally inches from the face and chest of our patient, meaning that he was basically staring into a loaded shotgun. One poor choice on our part and the airbag would deploy right into his compromised neck, chest, and face. It was scary and the stress was palpable.

We couldn't move the steering wheel which meant we couldn't take him out the left or right doors. The rear of the vehicle was now the only option.

A new critical issue was the fact that we had no idea if his neck and back had been fractured. We'd secured his neck with a C-Collar and even now we were working to get the KED[20] attached, thus securing his spine. Fortunately, the driver had sensation to his toes and could squeeze our hands, but if we cut the seat and laid it back would our driver be paralyzed?

While fire fighters debated the safest way to remove the driver, a flight paramedic reached through the right front passenger window and balancing at an odd angle started a large bore IV in our driver's right arm. He then attached a bag of IV fluids which he squeezed with his hands for rapid infusion.

It was about this time that a strange deep bass thumping sound began to approach from on high. Looking out the shattered windows I could see the tops of trees swishing and swaying, leaves blew in all directions and gusts of wind scooped up debris off the road and field making a mini dust storm. What on earth!

---

[20] Kendrick Extrication Device. Is a vest designed to wrap around the patient utilizing various straps and clamps that totally immobilize the spine.

I leaned to the right, looked up and could see the bottom of a huge US Army helicopter topping the trees and coming in for a landing. When I say coming in, I mean coming in like it was a "Hot LZ" right out of Vietnam! The guy flying that bird must've been having flashbacks because he brought that baby in quick and put her down with authority. Amazing to behold.

As firemen ducked their heads and turned away from the blasts of hot air slapping debris in their faces, I could see two helmeted soldiers in green flight suits running toward us with trauma bags. Yep! I wouldn't have been surprised to hear someone shout, "Annnnd Action! Roll em!"

We all stared in awe, what can I say, it was impressive and it's not every day that a civilian gets to see that up close and personal.

The first soldier to the van identified himself as an Army doctor. He asked for and received a quick report from our Chief on the status of the patient. Then a Fire Captain from the other department briefed the Doc about the concerns regarding the vehicle.

The Doc didn't hesitate, he turned toward the firefighter holding the hydraulic cutters and said, "Cut him out now! Cut the seat and take him out the back!"

Well, that was settled that in a hurry.[21]

The connecting joints of the seat were cut, and by this time the KED had been properly secured around our patient. The back of the seat was pulled free and out the window while myself, my Chief and other hands reaching from outside kept our driver in a sitting position, bracing his back.

Meanwhile the backboard had been pushed to me from the back window and we placed it as low to our patient's hips as we could get it. Then, after explaining to our driver what was about to happen, we told him, "Ok buddy, here we go. We're going to lay you back and this is really going to suck. I'm sorry."

All the while we moved the driver he screamed in pain. I looked down at his legs and could plainly see they were broken. He screamed as the muscles in his legs spasmed and shook. Reaching down he grasped the side of the backboard and shrieked otherworldly sounds.

---

[21] I don't mean to insinuate that the fire department personnel were ineffective and had reached a roadblock. The problem was a real one and there was not a person there who did not fully understand the ramifications on flippantly cutting the seat and pulling him through the rear of the van. The Army doctor shouldered all of that responsibility onto his shoulders in an instant, made the call and the deed was done, quite expertly.

I reached up and pried his hand loose of the backboard. He had inadvertently prolonged his pain in that we could not move him up the board while he clutched its side. With his hand free I grasped it hard and motioned for a firefighter reaching through the window to take the hand and bear the massive grip.

I then reached down, and both my Chief and I did our best to keep the legs as straight as possible, working to keep the inevitable swaying of the board to a minimum.

Finally! Our driver was fully on the backboard and as they prepared to move him out of the van, I looked up at his legs which now rested four inches from my face. It was those jagged ivory-colored bones poking through his blood-soaked jeans that spoke volumes.

In seconds I secured the strap over his legs and called out, "Bottom strap secure!"

In the next few moments, staring at those gruesome injuries, I truly began to respect the decision-making capabilities of a true veteran of EMS, our Chief. He had expertly made the calls and patched up the injuries by severity. He had staunched the flow of blood and made the scene secure from fire hazard. All while crammed in a smoking vehicle with a rookie behind him and a bloody pulp of a person in front of him.

Within a few minutes the green Army Huey was airborne and on its way to Wilford Hall Medical Center, Lackland Air Force Base. Our patient was on the way to expert state of the art help.

The Chief and I exited the back of the van, and it was then I noticed that the AirLife helicopter had also departed. I was amazed at how serene the scene had become. Of course, the sound of generators humming was still present, but it seemed almost like a lullaby compared to the audible thrashing we'd been under.

The setting had changed and so had my body. I had been running on adrenaline for quite a while and now I just crumpled next to the road. My legs were done. I removed my helmet and laid it on the rocky ground beside the road. I removed my jacket and wiped the sweat from my stinging eyes.

A bottle of water was handed to me, and I gulped it down in seconds. I lay on the ground with my head resting on my helmet. Looking up at the stars I reflected on everything we'd done. I thought of our patient and knew that his ordeal was long from over. I said a quick prayer for him and closed my eyes.

"Blocker. You did a good job tonight."

It was my Chief.

I sat up but he motioned for me to relax.

"Thank you. You too sir," was all I could muster.

We looked over the carnage and I looked up at his wrinkled weathered face wondering what his thoughts were. He said nothing, he just shook his head, looked down at me, smiled and said, "Well, come on, let's get back to the station."

A couple hours later I was back home and telling my family all about the accident scene, but I spared them many of the details that you've just read. A few minutes into my story the phone rang, and my mother answered, "Hello, Blocker residence."

I could tell by the ensuing conversation that it was a lady from church who had called. My mother let out a gasp and said, "Ok, we sure will. We will pray right now."

Hanging up the phone mom turned to us and said, "That was Mrs. Smith.[22] She just said her husband was in a terrible accident tonight and had been airlifted to Wilford Hall."

---

[22] A pseudonym for privacy sake.

I knew Mr. Smith very well from our church and went to school with his kids for years. I'd been in the vehicle with him for at least an hour and never even realized it was him! I couldn't recognize him because of the condition of his face. The whole time we were with him we'd just called him, "Sir." We never used his name or even asked it.

A couple weeks later I went up to the hospital and saw Mr. Smith who was beaming from ear to ear. He had tears in his eyes as he said, "I understand you were in the van with me. You saved my life."

I thanked him but said, "Mr. Smith, there was a whole team of people that saved you that night. I was just one of many."

He looked down at his legs which were propped up. I could see shiny pins sticking out of his legs in long rows. The bars attached to the pins gave the legs a robotic look.

Mr. Smith looked up at me and said, "Well, I'll say it again, thank you."

I smiled, "My honor sir."

Charley

On the 15th of August 1998 meteorologists based out of the National Hurricane Center in University Park, Florida noticed a small patch of what they called, "deep convection" a couple hundred miles northeast of the Virgin Islands.

To you and me this meant that a ton of hot air blowing out of the Sahara Desert riding the African Easterly Jetstream, met up with a ton of colder air in the upper troposphere. The mixing of hot and cold air created an unstable environment. In fact, it is out of just such convections that hurricanes are born.

This tropical storm was given the name Charley and he initially followed on the heels of his troublesome sister who would eventually become Hurricane Bonnie. It was Bonnie who would belt the East Coast of the US all the way up to Vermont. So, while Bonnie ventured north, her brother Charley meandered southwest.

On August 20th a US Air Force C-130 of the famed 53rd Weather Reconnaissance Squadron, (known as the "Hurricane Hunters"), lifted off from the tarmac at Keesler Air Force Base, Biloxi, Mississippi. Once airborne the pilot set a course for Charley. They would pierce the storm and determine its intent.

In an interview with Mike Brassfield of the Times, Jerry Jarrell, director of the National Hurricane Center, spoke of Charley intelligently using information provided him only minutes before by the Hurricane Hunters. So, what was Jarrell's take on the Charley, "It really flared up. It has come on like gangbusters today."

The description wasn't very scientific but absolutely everyone knew what it meant. Charley could be trouble.

Indeed, the message was understood for soon thereafter Tropical Storm warnings were posted from Galveston to Brownsville. It was anyone's guess where Charley would hit, but the target was sure to be Texas.

In response to the looming threat hundreds of oil rigs throughout the Gulf of Mexico were ordered evacuated.

Ian James of the Associated Press was curious what such an evacuation order would entail. Was it really a big deal? James was able to latch on to a Petty Officer Rusty Miller of the Coast Guard who set him straight, "There's a lot of rigs in the Gulf and each one has an average of 120 to 148 personnel."

Yeah, it was a big deal.

The reality was that Texas had seen its fair share of Tropical Storms and Hurricanes, so Charley didn't really stir up any fears. The storm never even achieved hurricane status on its approach to Texas. Truth be told, farmers and ranchers all over South Texas were excited knowing that the dried-up reservoirs, lakes, ponds and streams would finally receive some much-needed water.[23]

The storm imbued Texans with a sense of relief rather than dread. The front page of *The Victoria Advocate* on August 22nd euphorically exclaimed the headline, "Then Came Rain."

Residents in the South Texas town of McAllen awoke to find their newspaper[24] featuring several front-page stories about the wonderful news of coming rain. One journalist, Cindy Brown, printed a photo of a smiling young teenager crossing a street with her mother under an umbrella. The caption seemed to implore Charley to stop by for a visit. In bold half-inch letters the headline beseeched, "Hey Charley, What About Us?"

---

[23] The drought had been so bad that ranchers had to depend on hay donated from farms in Kansas.
[24] McAllen's newspaper was titled *The Monitor*.

A few inches above the photo was an article by journalist Gina Perales of the Harlingen *Valley Morning Star* titled, *"Charley could still help by dumping good rain in right places."*

Perales quoted Eddie R. Chapa, the Civil Defense director for Willacy County, "We haven't had rain in so long that we can probably handle a little more than we normally would. I hope we get some good rain."

Chapa's comments were thankful and sincere. The journalists themselves were all likewise overjoyed that rain was on the way. From the rancher to the farmer and the teacher to the journalist the news of rain was welcome. Especially since Charley was only a Tropical Storm and not a Hurricane.

The deep thirst of Texas was going to be quenched by Charley whether Texas liked the outcome or not.

Charley laboriously pushed ashore just south of Port Aransas and sluggishly moved across the hill country toward the border town of Del Rio. It was there, on the 23rd of August that Charley stalled, dropping sixteen inches of rain onto the unsuspecting sleeping city.[25]

---

[25] In a report filed on October 23rd, 1998, Edward N. Rappaport of the National Hurricane Center reported that the record had previously been 8.79 inches which was set on June 13th, 1935.

It rained…and rained…and rained.

Streets struggled to funnel the water into drainage grates. Culverts, trying to manage the flow, soon filled to capacity causing geysers of water to shoot up through manhole covers that clinked and clanked against the water's force. Ditches, soon overflowed into the streets. Creeks rose, brooks rose, and then the river rose. As the once clear and tranquil San Felipe crested its banks brown angry waters from the northwest converged with the San Felipe creating a rushing, churning wall of water that descended on thousands of homes.

"It hit us hard, it hit us fast," said Tracey Portillo who recounted the nightmare to Associated Press Writer Kelley Shannon. Tracey clung to her three-year-old son while water smashed walls and poured in through windows. Using a cigarette lighter she was able to negotiate the horrific scene and find safety. Speaking of her toddler she said, "He was scared of the thunder. Then I told him to think of the angels and he went asleep."[26]

Hearing and reading the accounts was heart-breaking. One woman told of her son placing his grandmother on top

---

[26] Shannon, Kelley, "Parched South Texas hit by deluge as storm hovers," Del Rio News-Herald, August 25, 1998 pg. 1,3.

of a sewing machine table because the water in their home had surged up to her neck.[27]

Long time Del Rio resident Jim Bob Hill recalled, "I heard people screaming from across the raging waters and realized that they were up in trees and on house roofs. I was urged to try and get my boat in the water and to attempt rescuing operations. I tried…I really tried…but the waters were raging by so fast, about 60 to 70 miles an hour."

Mr. Hill went to his porch and could hear his dad's goats bleating, "I went and got my dad and we walked to the pens. I told him to wait and shine the light while I looked to where I could hear the bleating. I went back to dad, and he said, 'Jim Bob those are people, not our goats.' I said, 'yes sir.'" [28]

Powerless to help, the two Hill men could only listen to the terrified human bleating and pray that those trapped would survive.

The power of the water was such that entire neighborhoods were destroyed. Houses, lifted off

---

[27] Ibid.
[28] Delgado, Rosa, "Jim Bob Hill recalls: 'It was a night from hell,'" Del Rio News-Herald, August 27, 1998, pg. 1 (all quotes from Mr. Jim Bob Hill come from this well written article)

foundations, were deposited onto the tops of bridges or simply smashed into splinters. There was little rescuers could do in such perilous conditions. Even those highly trained in water rescues were powerless against the smashing, churning strength of the press.

Mr. Hill summed it up best, "It was a night from hell."

As I lounged in my comfortably dry home watching the carnage on television, I began to feel that same calling, the identical nudge that came from within when I'd first seen the savage black columns of smoke in Oklahoma City only three years before.

However, this time I had the skills and experience that would help my community, so the following morning, August 26^{th,} I kept my word. I fulfilled a promise I had made on April 19, 1995, when staring at the handiwork of Timothy McVeigh. Every article of clothing I put on was a promise kept. I donned my EMT pants, my Medic One Ambulance shirt, grabbed my trauma sheers and my stethoscope and made my way over to the Red Cross HQ. I was going to just show up and offer my services. I needed them to recognize I had come to work and that I had a certain skill set.

It's funny, but no one knew what to do with an EMT who just showed up, asking to be put to work. A frazzled woman asked, "What would you like to do?"

I replied, "I'll do anything you need; I can work at an aid station, or I can lift boxes, packages or cases of water. I can be here all day. Just tell me what you want done and I'll do it."

Well, perhaps I should have given her a set job because my willingness to do anything seemed too much for her to handle so she passed me on to someone else. I guess my uniform made her feel that I would be better utilized in operations. Before I knew it, I was in the actual administration section of the fancy building and speaking to a fella who sported a fetching white Santa beard.

I introduced myself and spoke frankly, "I'll do anything you need. Just put me to use. You have me for a couple days."

The guy smiled, lifted his eyebrows and said, "Ok, well how 'bout I give you some keys and you drive one of our vehicles to Del Rio and run some errands for us?"

I was thrilled and accepted the job immediately.

After filling out some paperwork and thus becoming "official" I was given the keys to a brand new white 1998 Chevy Venture minivan which was even then being loaded with supplies for a shelter in Uvalde. It was on the way to Del Rio.

It seemed that every department had a representative talk to me about issues they needed handled or information they required. One fella from the Communications Department asked me to contact any HAM Radio operators working out of the Red Cross shelter and to, "Get their call signs and the frequencies." I was asked to do the same for Del Rio once I arrived there.[29]

With the van fully loaded I set off for the unknown. This was to be my first time working a natural disaster and I was both thrilled and terrified.

In Uvalde, I deposited the supplies they needed and contacted the radio operators as instructed. This entire process took only minutes, and I was quickly on my way to ground zero, Del Rio. A border town whose name eerily meant, "From the river."

---

[29] Amateur Radio Operators, called Ham operators, use radio sets to communicate across vast distances. They are essential during emergencies because the sets can be run off battery power and generators. There is almost always a way to get a message out when a Ham operator is nearby. When electricity fails, when cell towers go down the radio operators transmit messages to disaster relief organizations.

There were checkpoints along the way but the Red Cross placard on the side of the van granted me access to anywhere I needed to go. I found the shelter easy enough as it was the Civic Center.

Walking through the parking lot I was struck by how packed it was with vehicles. There were several large Semi's which were all in various stages of unloading. One trailer displayed the words, "Baptist Disaster Truck" while another one beside it belonged to the Seventh Day Adventists.

The famous Red Cross canteen trucks were parked side by side and I could see from whence they had traveled: Abilene (246 miles), Lubbock (350 miles), Wichita Falls (395 miles), Amarillo (454 miles) and of course San Antonio (158 miles).

Parked along with the canteen trucks was a US Air Force HUMVEE from Laughlin Air Force Base which boasted Del Rio as its home. The Air Force had sent a team of doctors, nurses, and medics. These outstanding women and men were overseeing the medical care of the destitute citizens, who having lost everything now called the shelter home.

When a few steps from the door I caught some motion out the corner of my right eye. There, only a few feet away, stood a teenage girl leaning over a trough and soaping up her hair. Beside her stood a young lady who looked to be the same age and who held onto a pitcher of water. Without being asked to do so, she began to pour the contents of the pitcher over her friend's soapy head. As I stepped through the door, I could hear them both giggling.

Inside I found the director of the facility who invited me to follow her around.[30]

At one point a lady walked up to the director, introduced herself as a representative of a local bank and then proceeded to deliver the news, "Our bank would like to help so I've been instructed to make ten thousand dollars available to you."

Such acts of kindness abounded.

It seemed that every few seconds someone was giving aid to the best of their means. One lady from Eagle Pass brought a load of 20 one-gallon jugs of water.

A tall Texan with a large cowboy hat introduced himself and with a drawl right out of Lonesome Dove said, "I'm from Uvalde. I brought along a trailer full of portable

---

[30] I wish I could remember her name but the journal I kept during this time makes no mention of any names. She was amazing and she knows who she is.

restrooms which I'm sure ya'll can use. We'll manage and pay for the upkeep of 'em."

About thirty minutes later the entire football team from Del Rio High showed up with their coach. The guys wore their practice jerseys and worked their butts off hauling boxes, cases of water and unloading whatever Good Samaritan trailers pulled up. It was darn inspirational to behold. Go Rams!

The meeting hall was converted into a temporary living quarters. Over a hundred cots were lined up and each seemed to have been claimed. A few folks tried to catch a nap, but it was pointless with all the children running around, playing.

There was a daycare, so that parents could begin filling out the paperwork for the various programs that would provide them financial assistance in the coming months. Councilors were there to guide families through these processes and pastors, priests and reverends made frequent rounds praying with folks but for the most part just providing a shoulder to cry on.

As I spoke to the staff members and volunteers, I wrote down the items they desperately needed. This would be provided to Red Cross Headquarters, back in San Antonio.

On my way out the door I said goodbye to the director and asked, "Would you like me to bring back anything special for you?"

She smiled and said, "Yeah, a bag of ice."

I grinned. It was a small luxury that we take for granted every day.

With that I was back in my vehicle and on my return trip to San Antonio, bearing only a mind and heart full of little dramas I had seen play out. Things that no one would ever know if I didn't record them.

So, later that night, I pulled out a black composition book and began to write about all the people I'd met, the acts of kindness I'd witnessed, and the coming together of a State. I was honored to have done my part, but I wish I could have done more. As it turned out I didn't provide any medical help that day, the Air Force had that area covered. However, I delivered supplies, wrote down the needs voiced by various staff members and department heads and then delivered this list to Red Cross Headquarters in San Antonio.

As I lay on my bed that night everything seemed to speak of Del Rio. My comfortable bed reminded me of those sleeping in the Civic Center. The chirping of the water sprinkler outside my window, hinted at the hospital in Del Rio that received their water from an 18-wheeler tanker truck. The red digital numbers of my alarm clock proclaimed that I had a life, while many did not.

The Alphas

It had only been a few days since I took part in the efforts to aid the flood victims of Del Rio, and now it was transition time. The date was August 31st, 1998, and it was to be my first shift in the Level One Trauma Center.

A few weeks prior, my paramedic partner aboard the ambulance had recommended I work there. We talked about it quite often and he convinced me to go in for an interview, allowing me to drop his name.

It worked, I had the job, but it would be a part time venture.

Now, it was my first shift and to say I was terrified would be putting it mildly. Adding to my anxiety a family friend coyly asked, "Why are you starting at a Level One Trauma Center? Why not work at a small ER and then go up to the big dogs?"

Well, I had no answer for that logical question. I guess I just was a "jump into the deep side of the pool" kind of guy.

I suspect that I knew how life changing this job would be because I decided to keep a journal.[31] Of course HIPPA laws kept me from documenting any patient identifiers, but I could at least jot down the juicy stuff. Yuck! Poor choice of words.

Shifts in the ER were generally doled out in 12-hour increments. Day shift was from 7am to 7pm and then "nights" came in to take the baton at 7pm to 7am and so on. There were occasional minor changes to that schedule, but it was true of the vast majority of the staff, of which there were many. In the ER alone we had over two hundred nurses, techs (medics), and clerks working all shifts at various times of the week.

As with any job boasting a large pool of employees you have your stars and your laggards. The stars shone brightly and the laggards, well, they are lost to history. They would disappear when crap hit the fan, and then show up breathless after everything had been handled. Incredible.

We began each shift with about thirteen RN's that included the Charge Nurse and PCC (Patient Care Coordinator aka Supervisor). In addition, there were about five ER Technicians who helped the nurses manage their patients. These techs were almost exclusively EMT's with

---

[31] So glad I did for it was a tremendous resource for this book.

tons of experience and many had seen combat in the Gulf War, Panama, and Somalia.

It didn't take long for me to learn that it was the RN's who made the ER run efficiently. Their greatest ability was multi-tasking. It was astounding to see them have so much dumped on them at one time and it seemingly not phase them.

Equally impressive was another ability forged by hundreds of hours in this environment; experience, time, sweat, fear, pain, and loss had taught them the phenomenal ability to anticipate the needs of the doctors, PA's, and their patients.

Dozens of times a day I witnessed this extreme awareness as multiple RNs were intelligently but also psychically aware of their patient's physical and emotional being.

This was an attribute I knew I would need to harness if I was to be a factor. Ah yes, that's the word that drove me every single day and night, "Factor."

I wanted to matter. The thought of doing the bare minimum made me sick to my stomach. I was there to learn, and I understood that the only way this would happen was by immersing myself into the cauldron.

I knew it was going to be uncomfortable for two obvious reasons: One, I was surrounded by Alphas and Two, I didn't know crap. I mean, I had a basic knowledge, but it was apparent to me within minutes that I would have to basically start from scratch.

One awkward example comes to mind. I recall being told to go to the Resuscitation Room and help. I walked in, wide-eyed and terrified. Peggy, handed me a syringe of blood and said, "Get me a Chem 13, CBC, PT, PTT, Type and Screen and run a quick Crit."

I stood there for what seemed like an eternity holding the syringe, tried to clear my dry throat, and feebly asked, "What are those?"

Peggy looked at me, smiled, pointed to the IV cart, and patiently said, "Spike that blood into a Blue Top, Purple Top, Green Top and Pink Top."

I spun on my heel and said, "Got it."

Ok, now colors I can understand. In the Fire Department we said such "Dumbing down of routines" was called making them, "Firemen proof."

So, you can imagine my discomfort knowing full well that though I looked the part, I didn't know jack. On top of this I knew full well that I was surrounded by a whole new breed of coworkers.

Each and every nurse who'd been there longer than six months had proved to be an alpha. Now, such was not the case for every nurse who applied for the job. Sure, they were brave to try, but I would see many nurses show up for a shift or two and never return. I saw one nurse last a single hour. It was just too much stress. Actually, looking back, perhaps she was just saner than the rest.

So, imagine my rookie-self, sporting pressed and creased blue scrubs, shiny new badge, and clean-shaven face showing up early for my first shift, ready to, "make a difference."

More than once, in the weeks that would follow, I thought that the Crocodile Hunter, Steve Irwin, should have done an episode in the ER. I could picture him gingerly stepping through the ambulance-bay doors, hunched over, looking left and then right, taking a few quiet steps forward, looking back at the trailing camera and whispering, "Crickey, have to be very careful here Mate, this is the land of the Alpha Female."

Anyway, when I stepped into the breakroom for my very first "Shift Huddle" everyone looked up at me with the hollowest eyes I'd ever seen. It was unnerving. I'd never seen such eyes before. What is that old saying, "The eyes are the window to the soul."[32] Well, looking into those windows made me swallow hard. Rough crowd. I seemed to be that one little fish who, oblivious to its surroundings, just blithely saunters through a school of barracuda. It's how I felt.

Minutes later I was officially introduced to the crew and a couple voices dryly muttered, "Welcome to Nam."

A few burned out souls laughed.

The Charge Nurse smiled and said, "Now, everyone be nice. We need the help."

A couple groans could be heard.

I smiled and wondered, "What have you gotten yourself into Blocker?"

---

[32] William Shakespeare

The Nam

The back of the green giant monster slowly opens revealing fresh new arrivals, new troops, replacements, "New Meat!" fresh from the States. The main character squints as tiny particles of burnt red dust blow into his face stinging his eyes. Our soldier wipes those eyes clear and blinks hard.

The scene is abysmally chaotic as these new arrivals bump up against the filthy and weathered "Old Timers" heading back to the US. It's a foreign land and a far cry from the cozy life only left hours before. A newly minted soldier with a Southern drawl says, "Oh man! Is that what I think it is."

Our soldier watches as several black body bags are roughly lifted one by one into the departing green monster, the C-130, that had just delivered this fresh new crop to the slaughter.

Suddenly we hear a voice call out, "Welcome to the Nam! Follow me!"

It's that famous line from the movie *Platoon* by Oliver Stone that somehow made its way into the recesses of the entire being of this Emergency Department. I knew the crew was joking around when they told me, "Welcome to Nam," but why had they chosen that particular phrase? They could have said, "You'll be sooooorrrrryyy" or, "Welcome to Hell." No, they chose a phrase that seemed to have a very personal meaning to it. It felt visceral.

"Welcome to Nam."

My stomach churned. I could feel a pit well up inside me.

Reflecting on that moment in the break room, I couldn't help but realize that this veteran crew had seen several lifetime's worth of horrendous stuff. They knew I would too.

These women and men had been battered day after day, night after night and they had survived the punishment for years. I could see it in the way they sat at the table. It was in the way they wore their uniforms and badges. Most importantly it was in their eyes. It was this last fact that terrified me.

The fictional character that tells the new arrivals, "Welcome to the Nam" was hard as nails. This crew was hard as nails.

Would I become…hard…as…nails?

Triage

tri·age
/trēˈäZH/

Origin: French

"trier" meaning "separate"
"triage" meaning "the action of sorting"

Ours was a county hospital and as such we dealt with both extremes of social classes as we know them today. In one bay lay a cracked-out prostitute, while on the other side of the curtain, lay a high-profile news reporter. We were like Jesus, we accepted everyone.

As we treated such a wide variety of patients, we had very tight security. In fact, to enter our registration area one had to pass through a metal detector that was manned by hospital security.

A testament to the effectiveness of the metal detector was the weekly cleanup of the bushes that would inevitably turn up a collection of discarded knives. Seems visitors would catch a glimpse of the detector, turn around, toss their knives, and then promptly forget about them. It was that kind of a place.

This front entrance to our department was known to patients as our intake and registration area. To those of us who worked there it was simply known as triage.

Assigned to work triage were our own clerks who were aggressive and testy. They dealt with phones that never seemed to be mute, stacks of paper that only grew, incoherent families with too many questions and juvenile med students perpetually breaking equipment. So, they were beyond niceties. For the most part our clerks were cordial, but always very correct in their interactions. No funny business.

Those who worked the front desk were nicknamed the "Door Nazis." This was a testament to their tight control over who was granted access through the doors that led to the back. We were thankful for their tenacity.

Then there were the nurses.

Triage is not a place for new RN's. It's where you place your nurses who are highly competent. They must also possess that amazing ability to cut to the chase very quickly.

As there's always a line of patients waiting to check in there's no time for a "Chatty Kathy" nurse. Succinct questions are the verbal scalpels.

"What brings you in today?"

"When did this pain start?"

"Is there anything that makes the pain worse?"

"Do you have any allergies?"

"Are you currently taking any medications?"

"Significant Medical History?"

Vital signs are usually checked during this question period to speed up the process. Speed is vital for we all know our patient's favorite question, "How much longer is it going to be?" is only moments from being uttered.

Sitting in that chair, asking those questions, laying eyes and hands on every patient is not an easy job. These RN's must make life and death calls, while knowing they have a limited number of beds available in the back, and an unlimited number of patients checking in.

I always admired the courage and professionalism of these nurses who knew that once they clocked in, they could look forward to a 12-hour shift being cajoled, ridiculed, harassed and cussed out by waiting patients and their visitors.

Somehow, these same RN's also managed to take EMS reports and help those looking for relatives. All while answering questions over their left shoulder and holding a thermometer in the mouth of a new patient to their right.

You might recall I mentioned that the place was full of Alphas. Well, it had to be. This was serious business.

However, even in this environment there were moments of levity in triage.

We had several clerks who were fluent in Spanish. I recall one such clerk, a Mexican American in her mid-fifties, who was extremely burned out. One night she was assigned the information desk. She fell further and further behind in her duties as several patients and their families plied her with questions.

Her stack of charts needing to be processed grew and her patience plummeted.

One lady approached the desk and asked, "Hablas espanol?"[33]

Our clerk, looked up at the lady and shook her head side to side and said, "No, I don't speak Spanish."

---

[33] "Do you speak Spanish?"

The lady wasn't buying it, so she asked again but this time said, "Estoy Seguro de que hablas espanol."[34]

Our clerk could have won an Academy Award for the blank stare she offered as reply.

The lady stomped off and our clerk continued filling charts and answering the phone and window.

"Beep! Beep! Beep!"

It was the phone. Our clerk robotically picks up the phone and in a monotone voice asks how she can help.

The caller asks in Spanish a series of questions to which our clerk replies in perfect, infallible Spanish.

The line was silent for a second and the lady in Spanish says, "So, you do speak Spanish. I am sitting a few feet from you watching you from the waiting area. You should be ashamed of yourself."

Oh My Gosh! As you can imagine the story spread like a wildfire through the ER. We laughed and laughed picturing the astonished looked on our burned-out clerk's face.

---

[34] "I am sure you speak Spanish."

So funny.

Referencing our clerks, one should know that it was their desk that was immediately seen when folks entered the ER. To the right was the triage station. Those who entered looked up at the signs and headed to either the "Information Desk" or "Triage."

If a patient walked up to triage, they were registered and immediately asked their main reason for coming into the ER. We call this the "Chief Complaint." It's not used in a negative context. It's just the reason the patient is there, and if you were a fly on the wall you might hear the following conversation between the triage nurse and our new patient.

Triage Nurse: "Ok Mr. Doe have a seat right there and I'll get your vital signs and your reason for being here."

Mr. Doe: "Thank you."

Triage Nurse: "So, Mr. Doe, what brings you in today?"

Mr. Doe: "Well you see I have this pain right here in my abdomen."

Triage Nurse: "On a scale of zero to ten, with ten being the worst pain imaginable what number would you give this pain?"

Mr. Doe: "Oh, it's definitely a twenty."[35]

Triage Nurse: "Ok, and when did this pain start?"

Mr. Doe: "I would say about six years ago."

The nurse never changes her expression. She stares at the computer screen typing in the information.

Triage Nurse: "Ok and what makes today worse than the past two thousand one hundred and ninety days?"

The line is said with flat affect indicating not the slightest hint of emotion. The patient stirs in the chair, squirming a bit, trying to comprehend if the nurse is sarcastic or just a wizard.

Mr. Doe: "Well, it got worse today."

Triage Nurse: "Ok, when was the last time you ate?"

---

[35] This guy is already annoying to the nurse because the parameters were clearly zero to ten. There is no possibility of anything higher than a ten. Anyway, forgive my digression.

Mr. Doe: "About an hour ago. I stopped at a Burger King on the way here."

Triage Nurse: "All right, Yes, I can see your large Burger King cup there. Let's go ahead and throw that away because they're probably going to do a CT of your abdomen. Let's just hope nothing serious is going on because since you ate on the way here it'll delay any procedures for eight hours."

The RN charts, "*Pt arrived with large Burger King drink in hand and stated that he had eaten a Whopper with Cheese and Large Fries on the way to the ER. Pt has been instructed to discard his drink and to refrain from eating or drinking anything else until notified it is ok to do so. Pt has discarded the drink and states he understands the instructions given him.*"

Mr. Doe: "How long do you think I will be here?"

Triage Nurse: "Well, your care begins now, and you will soon see a PA who will initiate your orders."

Mr. Doe: "Ok, but how long do you think I will be here?"

Triage Nurse: "It's hard to say Mr. Doe. It could be a couple hours or all night. It just depends on what they discover."

Mr. Doe: "Well, how many people are ahead of me?"

Triage Nurse: "We don't take people back by time. We are of course mindful of how long people are waiting, but the more serious cases go first."

Mr. Doe: "Ok, thank you."

About forty-five minutes later Mr. Doe is seen at the vending machine, hunched over grabbing a candy bar from the dispensing slot. He then side steps and inserts a dollar bill into the other machine. He pushes a button and out pops a Dr. Pepper.

The triage nurse shakes her head, pulls up Mr. Doe's file and types, *"Against instructions the patient was just seen by me purchasing a candy bar and Dr. Pepper from the vending machine and is now consuming both at his seat in the waiting room. Pt is waiting for blood draw and urinalysis at this time."*[36]

---

[36] These vending machines were reviled by the nurses. It seemed wrong to offer candy and soda to patients with diabetes and health issues. The nurses won their argument and the machines were removed from the ER waiting room.

Such a scene played out day after day.

With a waiting room full of patients anxious to go back to a room, it was the triage nurses responsibility to know who their "sickest" patients were. Patients moved up and down that list depending on who entered the door. I can assure you that Mr. Doe would have moved DOWN the list especially with so many "Chest Pain" patients with risk factors coming in.

In addition to two nurses there was also assigned to triage a Tech/Medic whose job entailed drawing blood, attaining EKGs, and taking folks to the back once rooms opened up for them. There were of course many other tasks, but these were the primary ones.

In addition to the front entrance there was also our Ambulance Bay Doors. It was through these doors that passed the worst cases I'd see. They arrived by ambulance, helicopter, private vehicles and sometimes patients even knocked on the doors.

Gang bangers would often drive up, dump the bodies of their buddies and with tires screeching flee the ambulance drop-off area. It was the wild west. Sometimes though they'd pull up to the ambulance drop off and having reached their destination, pass out from loss of blood.

We'd pull out the bodies while the police pulled out the guns.

These were tricky because they were also crime scenes. We yanked the bodies out quickly, placed them on stretchers and tried our best to save them. Sometimes we did, other times we couldn't.

As we were a county, and thus government hospital we also took care of the prisoners from all the local jails and penitentiaries. In addition, we were tasked with medically clearing all of those taken into custody by Police but refused by the Magistrate until medical clearance had been attained. These all arrived first to triage. This made for an interesting dynamic. Orange jumpsuit prisoner sitting next to a grandma with chest pain.

Our ER had its own Psychiatry Department complete with a lockdown unit. This peripheral unit was always bustling. It's impact on our main ER was that these patients almost without exception required medical clearance before they would be accepted by Psychiatry. These also first came through triage.

Prisoners. Drunks. Grandma with Chest Pain. Psych patient on a meltdown. Quite the setting.

Let me set the scene.

When I would walk in the Ambulance Bay Doors at night to clock in, I would glance over at the Waiting Room Status Board, and it would almost always be filled to capacity.

I'd then look to see the wait time for the next person to go back and most days it would be upward of twelve hours. I had even seen over twenty hours a couple times.

This of course meant that the waiting room was full, with upward of seventy-five people waiting to go back to get seen by a doctor or PA.

In the triage waiting area I witnessed a lady who was with a relative who had become ill while visiting from out of town. She harrumphed her way up to the triage window and yelled at the RN, "This is ridiculous! I have been here two hours waiting to go back! How much longer is it going to be?"

An old lady, who had a quilt draped over her legs, sat knitting some socks (not kidding) and without looking up, shook her head from side to side and said, "Honey, you just got started. I've been here ten hours waiting."

The angry woman could see the knitting utensils, the ball of yarn, the quilt from home and knew she was in a whole new world. Welcome to the county ER.

It was in this environment that day after day, night after night, doctors, PA's, RN's, Medics and Clerks worked themselves to an early grave. Yet, we came back night after night to do it all over again.

When I first started working in triage it seemed chaotic, unbearable, the strain of it all. Then you learn from those around you that the goal is not to empty the waiting room for that will never happen. The goal is to provide excellent care to those in your charge. Don't look at the whole picture. Focus on your team, your assignment. Let the Charge Nurse worry about the broad goals of the night.

In this regard I'm reminded of the old story of the father who walked alongside his son on the beach. Covering the shore were thousands and thousands of starfish that had washed up and were stranded. One by one the father picked them up and threw them back into the sea.

The little boy with a quizzical look asked, "Why are you doing that? You're not going to make a difference."

The father smiled, picked up another starfish and tossed it back into the water. As he did so he turned to his son and said, "It makes a difference to that one."

Learning Curve

For the first two months that I worked in the ER I was discouraged. My preceptors were too busy to teach me, so I was having to learn by screwing up and this of course sucks.

At first, I just dealt with it because that's what I was raised to do. Don't complain. Move on.

That really stinks when its day after day and you're not improving. I mean, people's lives were on the line and all I needed was for someone to provide me an appropriate orientation, a proper tutor.

I was sick to my stomach, dreading every shift. My work ethic was kicking my butt and my learning curve seemed to become wider and longer. This was a whole new world from working on an ambulance.

RN: "Dennis, can you please go to bed number five and put a sugar tong on Mr. Lopez's right arm?"

Dennis: "Sure thing."

Dennis' Mind: "What the heck is a sugar tong?"

A quick trip to the computer station, a covert Google search, "What is a sugar tong?" Then, off to bed five I'd go, ready to apply the required splint.

RN: "Dennis, can you get me some tilts on bed twelve please?"

Dennis: "Sure thing."

I'd approach a fellow ER Medic and ask, "Tom, what the heck are tilts?"

Tom would smile and explain the process in taking the blood pressure of the patient as they lie flat, sit up and then stand.

Day after day it was like this. I was slowing my teams down and it drove me nuts.

The Blocker family takes pride in a strong work ethic. It's instilled into us that we are Blockers and that our name means reliability, patriotism, strength, compassion, friendliness, dependability, and honor.

During those first few months I detested myself. I seemed to always need a nurse to tell me what tasks to perform. Reactive, not proactive. I felt that I was a monkey just performing tricks. My mind was stalled, and I couldn't seem to get it started. I was not fulfilling my desire to be a factor.

I longed for the day when an RN would look up, see that I was assigned to her/his team and smile knowing their back was covered. That seemed to be way off in the distant future.

My paramount problem was that I didn't know what to anticipate. It wasn't enough to know how to take a blood pressure and how to draw blood. It didn't matter that I could perform a physical assessment if I didn't know what tubes to get for the ordered blood samples.

I wanted to take it a step further. If I was asked to get a red top, blue top, and lavender top blood tests I wanted to know why I was getting the samples and what each tube was testing.

A monkey can get a green top blood vial from the IV cart. However, only a good medic can get a green top because he knows the doctor ordered a Chem 10 on the patient in bed 23.

A chimp can get a blue top from an IV cart but only a top-notch medic knows that a blue top will be required because the Doc ordered a PT/PTT.

Taking it another step further, I wanted to know why I was checking a patient's Creatinine level before they had a CT with contrast.[37]

To start tackling these issues I took a splinting class so I would no longer need to research a Sugar Tong or an Ulnar Gutter. If a Doc asked for a Thumb Spica or a Long arm posterior splint well, I would know exactly what was required.

My experiences during this time greatly impacted how I trained others in the future. I would be hands on with my Padawans[38], always guiding, ever present, encouraging, testing, and teaching things that I had learned the hard way, on my own.

The learning curve was never more prominent than when I was assigned to the Trauma Room.

No lie, I'd get diarrhea when I would see my name assigned to that unit. I was terrified because I knew that these patients had mere seconds to live, and my knowledge base was minimal.

---

[37] Checking a patient's creatinine level reveals the fact if they have proper kidney function. If they do not have good kidney function, the administration of contrast into the IV could exacerbate an existing kidney issue.

[38] A Star Wars reference. Look it up. Yes, Stephanie is THE Padawan.

To prepare myself I'd often step in to help even though I was assigned to other units. As the medics set up the Level 1 Rapid Infuser my eyes watched every step, remembering. I'd take mental notes as the Pleur-evac chest drainage system was assembled and prepared for use.

With intense scrutiny I watched as the sterile trays were setup by medics who seemed to anticipate their need before called for. How did they know to do that? What were the ques from the trauma surgeons that alerted these awesome medics that a Chest Tube or DPL[39] tray were going to be needed?

If there was downtime (rare for sure) I'd make my way over to Trauma and pick the brain of the medics and nurses working in there. I'd offer to do the checklist for the room because in doing so I had to physically find each and every item in the room. I did this repeatedly until I got to the point I would instantly know where a Cook Catheter or a 32 French Chest Tube were located.

Need a Triple Lumen or an 8.5 Cordis? I'm your man. I know right where they are. I'll even have two pairs of sterile gloves in your preferred size on top, ready for you.

---

[39] A surgeon makes a small incision in the abdomen just below the umbilicus (belly button). A catheter is introduced through the incision into the abdomen. Saline is infused into the abdomen through the catheter, and then removed. If blood is present it is highly probable there is a serious intra-abdominal injury

If a patient has bilateral diminished breath sounds I immediately know to hook up a "Y" connector to the suction canister. In this configuration both Pleur-Evacs[40] will pull suction, and I'll still have one canister remaining so that the doctor can clear the airway with a suction tip as they intubate.

These were all lessons I had learned from watching the best and making a pest out of myself. I hungered for information. Anything that made me more effective was something I yearned for.

Gradually the anxiety began to vanish. Day after day I increased my library of knowledge. Then I attained wisdom that became my fuel for anticipation. The most important gift one can have in the ER is the ability to anticipate.[41]

My nervousness in Trauma would truly never go away, but I soon classified that nervousness in the same realm as nerves before a big basketball game. Once the clock started, I was solid.

---

[40] A sealed canister that is hooked up to suction on the wall and then connected to a chest tube inserted into the chest. The device removes air or blood trapped in the pleural cavity, thus allowing the lung to expand and fill with oxygen.

[41] A fact so important I have mentioned it many times within these pages.

In later years I would tell my trainees, "Use the nervous feeling in your gut to make you sharp. Let the adrenaline focus your mind on the report given by EMS. Clip note the main points. Prioritize them and prep your room accordingly."

It was arduous but my learning curve was something I had to endure. Like the butterfly emerging from its chrysalis, I had to endure the hardships to attain my true potential.

To become a factor.

Bridges

During my early years working ER I was amazed at how much tension there was between the ER and seemingly every other floor in the hospital. This was especially true for those who worked in the OR and the SICU.

Originally, I believed such horrible relations between departments was just an anomaly found only in my first hospital, the Trauma Center. However, when I subsequently moved to two other facilities, I found the same friction existed.

Is it the same everywhere?

Some of these bad feelings I understood as just good old-fashioned rivalry, which is good. It keeps competition high which makes outcomes better for our patients.

But there was also the fact that we in the ER offload our patients onto every department in the hospital. Of course, this is our job. We must keep patients moving. However, I know that the Emergency Department has earned some of this wrath in the admission process.

For example, sometimes the ER staff would transport a patient to let's say, the 8th floor. The patient's linens, gown and diaper would be completely soiled. The nurse or ER Tech/Medic would move the patient to the pristine bed, pull the rails up and then return to the ER.

The receiving nurse would naturally be appalled.

I made a mental note of this and anytime I took someone upstairs who was dirty I always stayed to help clean them up. I never dumped and ran.

So, in that regard, I could see how nurses on the floors who were already overwhelmed grew irritated about taking on the ER's patients.

By far though, the most intense rivalry is between the ER and the ICU. Maybe it's because they are both tribes of Alphas. The rivalry reminded me of the relationship that the Lakers and the Celtics had with each other in the 1980s and 1990s.[42] It was intense. As was the disdain felt between the ER and ICU.

I don't know when all the bad feelings started but it seemed to be a generational thing that had been passed on

---

[42] Those were some amazing games to watch. I was lucky to have witnessed the greatness of Magic Johnson, Larry Bird, James Worthy, Dennis Johnson, Byron Scott, Kevin McHale, Michael Cooper, Robert "The Chief" Parish, Kareem Abdul Jabar, Danny Ainge, Kurt Rambis, A C Green and others.

through the years. For all I know it started with Florence Nightingale and some nurse named Ingrid Lemke.

Now, I know there are many reasons to have a scowl. Especially if you are taking report from a bunch of cranky ER nurses. I also know that the endless scenes of death can get overwhelming in both the ER and the ICU.

A part of me wondered if it was just something passed on to the new hires during orientations in both departments. I just found it incredibly sad that so many nurses go to these units and seem to be influenced by the veteran nurses who bestow their bitterness onto the new crop.

Having said all of that I made a point to win over as many nurses as I could. From a strategic viewpoint, I could never understand making rivals with those you're going to do business with.

I didn't want to get into a situation where I needed a favor but couldn't go anywhere above the ER because all those bridges had been burned. To combat this, I worked very hard at building my own bridges. I guess you could say I became an engineer. I encouraged every new hire that I trained to be darn sure they never pissed off anyone from any of the hospital wards. I would take my padawan on trips to various floors and introduce them to my friends scattered all over the hospital.

It was a beautiful thing for if I needed some colostomy supplies, I knew I could walk up to the 10th floor and ask for some. If I needed some help trying to find our missing monitor leads, I could go to any department that received monitored patients and get help locating the missing leads.

This practice extended to hospital support staff as well. I'd learned the codes to housekeeping's closets and would pick up a broom and start sweeping up our messes. With mop in hand, I'd clean up a spill.

Environmental services personnel would enter the room, apologize, and attempt to take the mop. "No," I'd say, "it's ok. I got this. Why don't you go to the break room? Someone just ordered a bunch of sandwiches from Jason's Deli. Go grab something, I'll take care of this."

Sure, it was nice to help, and it sure made me feel good, but it also stored up coupons for future use.

This was respect for the team. Regard for the job those on the other floors were doing. Fulfillment of our mission. All of us were there to take care of patients and we needed each other to get the job done efficiently and safely.

Imagine a hospital where every department and ward have each other's back. How efficient would operations run if the employees saw themselves as individual cogs in a vital machine? Would efficiency and thus productivity rise if each employee worked at building bridges between floors and not burning them down?

For those readers who are thinking of healthcare in the Emergency Department I hope you'll be your own person. Don't fall into those time loops in which departments get stuck disliking other floors for reasons no one can really make sense of.

Build bridges. You'll be happier and it will only improve the efficiency of your goal to heal those who come into your care.

Part Two

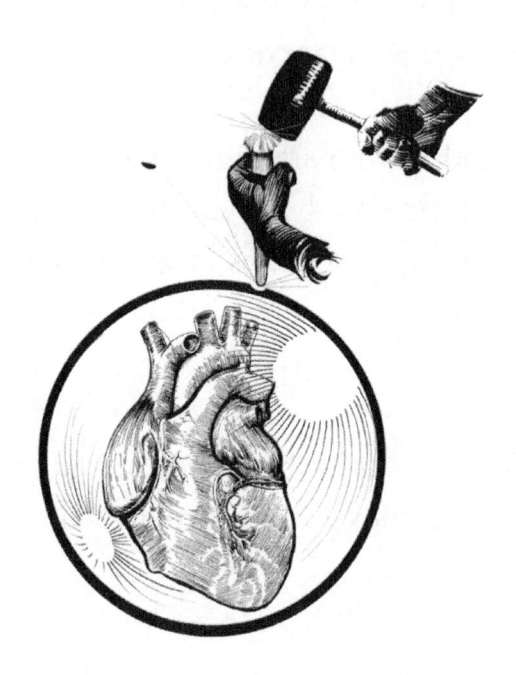

Trauma.

WARNING: Part Two has specific descriptions of medical trauma cases. If you have trauma, PTSD or you are recovering from emotional issues, this section may trigger you. Feel free to skip forward to Part Three. The author truly does not wish to further traumatize anyone.

Comfortable

At long last I finally began to feel more comfortable in the Trauma Center. I had a good grasp of what was expected, and I felt confident that I'd be an asset to the department. Now, don't get me wrong, the mere thought of going into the actual Trauma Room still terrified me. However, the regular operations of the ER were now routine.

With this new phase and a new career ahead of me I buckled down and prepared for whatever might come. I was soon to discover that there was just no way I could prepare for what would pass through the doors over the next several years.

Some of those stories, follow now.

The Lawsuit

One night, walking down the corridor between pods, I noticed a guy who'd been four point restrained to a stretcher in the hallway. The sight was nothing new as our facility had more than enough crazies to go around.

This dude was yelling, jerking, lunging, and cursing up a storm. I avoided looking at the guy hoping against hope that he'd let me pass without comment. No such luck.

As I entered his field of vision he called out to me, "Hey! You! I'm going to sue you! I'll have your job!"

I didn't know this guy and had no idea why he was restrained. The first time I'd seen him was this very moment, but no matter.

I answered, "Oh, really, you're going to sue me?"

He paused, looked me up and down, checking out my shoes, watch and scrubs. Having sufficiently given me the "once over" he lay back on the stretcher, exhaled and flatly said, "Nah, you don't look like you have anything."

I laughed. He was right, but I had one thing going for me, I wasn't tied to a stretcher.

Hammer Time

One evening the cops brought in this guy who looked like he'd been worked over pretty good. Several scarlet rivulets of blood coursed down his face, etching his nose and mouth.

The guy was handcuffed and still trying to head butt the police officers that brought him in. Of course, no one wanted this dude's bloody head connecting with any part of their own body, so we kept a distance.

Placed on a gurney the guy began bashing his head against the rail. Well now we had no choice, we had to step in.

We tried reasoning with him, but it was of no use. One of the officers mentioned that the guy had taken a hammer and struck himself (quite hard) in the head several times.

As the story is being related to us this dude is screaming, "I don't know why she broke up with me! Why! Why did she break up with me bro!"

Well, let me take a wild guess.

Down Mexico Way

Growing up in a Baptist family we were not allowed to watch movies with cursing. This left me and my sisters with movies that were either produced by Disney or from the 1930s, 40s, and 50s.

One of my favorites back then were the singing cowboy movies of Roy Rogers and Gene Autry. I liked him the best. *Down Mexico Way*, which was released in 1941, was one of my favorites.

Back when I was a kid in the mid 1980s, we'd travel from San Antonio down to Laredo, a border town, and cross into Mexico. We'd eat amazing food, search out jumping beans and mom would do some shopping. We loved it. There was something so cool about having another country so close to our own home.

Later, just before sunset, we'd recross the International Bridge over the Rio Grande, pile into our Ford Escort, and head back to San Antonio. I'd look out my window, rest my head against the frame of the door, feel the wind lash my face and I'd squint and stare as the sun set in the West. The orange sky, scrub brush, and fields of prickly pear brought to mind the Gene Autry song from the movie of the same title that I loved so much, *Down Mexico Way*.

South of the border, down Mexico way
That's where I fell in love when stars above came out to play
And now as I wander, my thoughts ever stray
South of the border, down Mexico way

It was all very romantic back then for Mexico was a place of wonder to explore. Vaqueros, Cowboys, Charreadas, Rodeos, great food, tremendous shopping. But that was years ago, days that are long gone. Where once there were sprawling ranches there are now compounds where drug lords reign. Once upon a time we could cross and have a blast but now the threat of kidnapping is too great. The cost too high to risk a visit.

It was during this growing environment of border town crime that our hospital found itself responsible for over thirty counties in South Texas. Several of these; Val Verde, Kinney, Maverick, Webb, Zapata, Hidalgo, Starr, and Cameron all border Mexico. As such, we saw many injuries related to illegal immigration, human trafficking, and drug wars.

I recall one night shift we received two US Federal Agents by helicopter who'd been ambushed in Nuevo Laredo, Mexico.[43] The men never stood a chance. Their

---

[43] This is the border town in Mexico that is a sister to Laredo, Texas on the US side of the Rio Grande River.

vehicle had been riddled with bullets as had their bodies. In fact, truth be told, they were dead before they arrived at our facility. They were Federal agents, so we worked them anyway. We showed them that respect.

Our proximity to the border meant that we also received a significant number of illegal immigrants who were unsuccessful in their bid to cross the rugged South Texas Plains.

The water starved region is home to roving bands of coyotes, one million feral hogs, the secretive but hungry mountain lion and the occasional bobcat. If the undocumented immigrant survives the wildlife, they must also survive the insects.

Texas bugs are varied and usually enormous. Almost every square inch of Texas soil is scoured by fire ants which are ravenous hunters willing to bite and sting repeatedly. Trouble is that they love to undertake such festivities with large groups of their friends. They are social beings.

Seeking shade under a blackbrush shrub might bring relief from the searing sun, but the shaded soil will almost assuredly be inhabited with these darn ants. Everyone in the state has their favorite fire ant stories to tell and they always end with clothes coming off in a hurry.

One mustn't forget the ten species of rattlesnakes that inhabit this region. These reptiles love the shade and are fond of lying in the crevices of rock clusters. Particularly places that those on foot would choose for a place to step.

In addition to the rattlesnakes there are the incredibly aggressive water moccasins (cotton mouths) that inhabit what few places where water can be found. Their venom is highly toxic and the fact that they're always in a rotten mood makes them one of the most reviled snakes of Texas.

Remember that scene from Lonesome Dove when the cowboy crosses a stream and thinks he's into some barbed wire? His buddies discovered it was water moccasins. Well, though they don't congregate like that I can attest to the fact that they're extremely aggressive.[44]

Add to that mix the venomous coral snakes and copperheads and you begin to understand why Texans wear cowboy boots.

If that isn't dangerous enough you can add scorpions, giant centipedes, killer bees, and a wide variety of plant life that is covered in thorns, thistles, and stinging vines.

---

[44] When I was a teen I had a harrowing three hour nocturnal encounter with multiple water moccasins along the Frio River. In our family the story is called "The Night of the Moccasins."

If you manage to survive all those hazards you still must deal with the unrelenting sun which, as stated before, unfortunately coincides with a killing lack of water sources.

It's a mixture not for the faint of heart.

When I think of those stout-hearted trekkers enduring all of those hardships to get to this country and a better life, I feel that they should have a prize at the end of the trail. I mean, there should be a certificate of citizenship waiting for them. If you're tough enough to survive all of that well then you have the stuff that Americans are made of.

Now, down here in South Texas there's a term for a person who smuggles illegal immigrants across the border. They're called, "Coyotes."

They are paid a fee to get these folks into Texas but if it appears they may be caught by Law Enforcement or the US Border Patrol, well, sometimes high-speed chases ensue.

I recall one night we had about four or five undocumented immigrants from Mexico come in by helicopter. In this case the Coyote was trying to elude the Border Patrol in a highspeed chase. Such an undertaking was frivolous for the lack of roads and the long stretches of open spaces.

Other law enforcement agencies were called, and blockades set up. This guy didn't have a chance to escape. As he tried to swerve around a roadblock the momentum caused him to lose control. His van toppled over and began to flip. The momentum wrenched the back doors open and humans began to eject at odd angles.

One poor man flew right into a tree and broke several bones in his arms and legs. Another guy went headfirst into a large bristling patch of prickly pear cactus.

Some of the immigrants had died on scene but the ones who came to us recovered and were sent back to Mexico. I well recall the two med-students who were tasked with pulling out the thousands of tiny barbs that pierced that one poor guys body. They were at that job for hours. One at a time. Removing those little stickers with tweezers.

I recall another fella who, when he was discovered, was extremely dehydrated. His lips were cracked and bleeding, his eyes sunken back into his skull. The poor guy had tried jumping onto a train that was passing by. It was a good idea as it would have taken him to a large city where he could get water and perhaps make some connections. However, in his weakened condition when he went to reach for the railing on the side of the car, he lost his balance. Sprawling forward his right leg slid under the wheels and was promptly cut off.

Lying there along the tracks he would have bled to death, but he deftly removed his belt and made a tourniquet which worked wonderfully. The Texas sun has no sympathy though and it continued to burn his skin and sap the last vestiges of energy he had.

Mercifully he passed out. This fella would have died were it not for a rancher who was driving an ATV, checking his fence lines. EMS was called, a helicopter was sent, and the guy was saved. The guy looked horrible but was in good spirits. He was glad to be alive.

A bunch of us were putting together an order to be picked up at a local Mexican Restaurant, Taco Cabana. Our new amputee had surgery scheduled for the morning so he could not eat anything after midnight. However, he still had an hour to go so we asked him if he'd like some tacos.

I'll never forget that smile. It was the first we'd seen. The designated runner soon returned with the bag of goodies, and we passed them around. We sat huddled around talking with this guy, asking about his journey. We were curious about the contents of his pant pockets which contained over a dozen different kinds of rocks. They were a beautiful assortment but an unnecessary load.

He smiled and said that he'd been collecting them because they were beautiful, and it gave him something to occupy his mind. Well, I bagged them all up and secured them in our valuables closet so that he could have them when he went to his room. The guy was a tough hombre.

Stories like these were common. Folks trying to get to America and facing horrendous horrors and dangers at the hands of unscrupulous crooks who cared only for themselves.

Even recently here in San Antonio a semi-truck trailer had been found to contain dozens of immigrants. The truck was left in a Wal-Mart parking lot and unfortunately the air condition unit in the back had failed. The summer heat topped 100 outside and soon one by one these folks began to die.[45]

Such stories happen all over South Texas and it's not getting any better. Sure, there are criminals trying to get into our country, but there are also some very courageous, hardworking, freedom loving people who will face hell

---

[45] It was July 23rd, 2017, and nine people died in the back of that trailer. In 2003, in Victoria, Texas a similar incident happened but that time 19 people died.

itself just for the chance to be an American. Our country has some hard decisions to make, that's for sure, but that's also another book for someone else to write.

For me, when I look back on those days of my youth, I still see that orange sky, the rusty old train track along the highway, the jack rabbits at full flight. It's all there in my memories. But now there are these new memories of Mexico. The dark memories that bring melancholy.

Oh, for those days of long ago. Will we ever see them again, Down Mexico Way?

Tough Customers

Some patients were memorable for their unbelievable stupidity. Others because they seemed to be the unluckiest on the planet. A few stood out for their shear grit and mental toughness. They were impressive to behold.

One evening we got a lady who'd been riding on a tractor with her boyfriend. She admitted to us that she'd been drinking and that this may have contributed to her loss of balance.

She toppled off the back of the tractor, flipped over and went feet first into the baler. Her fast-acting boyfriend was able to stop the machine as it was mid-thigh on her.

As you can imagine, her legs were absolutely decimated.

The boyfriend sprang to action removing her belt and tying it around one stump that he untangled from the machine. He then used his belt on her other floppy stump.

With her free of the machine the boyfriend told her, "Sweetheart you're gonna have to hold your legs while I carry you."

He rolled them up and she held them as he carried her to the truck.

She was a trooper.

When she came into the trauma bay she was still holding those stumps that were connected by fibrous tissue here and there and mixed in hay, dirt and grime. There was absolutely no integrity to her legs. They were like noodles. Incredibly, she was the perfect vision of calm. It seemed like no big deal to her.

Of course, she lost those legs, but I have a sneaky suspicion that those amputations didn't slow her down in the least.

Speaking of slowing down, there is one crowd that never will, the hard-core motorcyclists.

This poor guy we received was riding a scenic hill-country route when some schmuck pulled out in front of him. The rider didn't have a chance. Smashing into the right front of the engine compartment propelled this guy over the hood.

The first parts of his body to connect with the ground were his hands, which he extended to cushion his fall. When the forward motion and the patient's weight were combined in earnest onto his wrists they instantly snapped. Both the ulnar and radius bones of both arms immediately punched through his skin. It was a shocking sight to see this man's hands resting beside his protruding arm bones.

As the tension was no longer on the muscles and tendons they began to spasm, causing this dude an intensity of pain seldom rivaled. Large beads of sweat rolled down the sides of his cheeks and forehead but he would not cry out in pain. He refused.

Our ortho Docs came down to see him. Maybe it was just the times but these ortho resident doctors, who were all in their mid to late 20's, seemed to have an aversion to ordering pain meds. I guess because they would then have to Document them.

For our motorcycle guy's pain they ordered 1mg of morphine which was like spitting on a fire. No effect at all. The nurses would give an appropriate dose and then tell the ortho resident, "Hey you need to write for 5 on that bilateral wrist guy."

The ortho Doc would hem and haw and the nurse would interject, "No, you NEED to write for 5 on that guy. His bones are sticking out of both arms and the muscles are spasming."

They always signed off on such orders but sometimes the order sheet was filled out by the nurse. She'd plop the Document down in front of the Doc and say, "I need your signature on this order sheet for the meds you ordered."

One thing about Trauma Center nurses, they're not afraid to speak their mind on behalf of their patients.

So, now it's time to reduce[46] these fractures.

The Ortho Docs gathered, and it suddenly hit me that there must have been a requirement that all ortho types be over six feet tall and male. Anyway, these guys gather and while one pulls down on the wrist, the other pulls up on the hand.

Meanwhile our patient's arm is spasming, so the Docs are now sweating as they try to pull these muscles and bones. There are no screams from our guy, only deep guttural grunts, like a body builder lifting weights.

By this time sweat is pouring down the foreheads of the both the Docs and our patient. Shucks, sweat was pouring down my forehead and I was only standing there should they need supplies. They just about had the position right,

---

[46] To manually put these bones back into their proper place.

but a flap of skin was catching on a bone, preventing the hand from sliding back over on top of the wrist.

One of the perspiring doctors exclaims, "Quick! Give me your shears!"

I hand him my shears, perplexed as to his intended use of them.

The Doc shoves the end of my shears into the arm and flips the skin flap under. In an instant the hand was now resting back where it was supposed to be.

Everyone was exhausted. Especially our patient.

The Doc then says the dreaded words, "Ok. Time for the other one."

Oh man, this sucks.

The patient calls out, "Wait! Wait! Wait! Let me make a phone call first."

I have the guy's cell phone, so I punch in the numbers he gives and press the phone against his left ear. I wonder who he needs to call at this most inopportune time.

Someone on the other end picks up and our guy says, "Hey Rick, hey this is John. I won't be making it in to work today. I'm in the hospital."

What a great guy! He takes the time to call in so another driver can be arranged to manage the delivery route. The nurses are impressed, and one says, "John, can I talk to your boss and explain why you're not coming in? You're too humble man. Your boss needs to know what you've been through and how awesome it is that you would take time to call in."

John agrees and the nurse fills in Rick who is astonished. Needless to say, his standing with that company improved significantly.

What a tough hombre.

The Nursing Home

One evening, around 3am, we received a call from San Antonio Fire Department. They had multiple units rescuing residents of a nursing home that was in the process of burning down. Many residents had died on scene, but we were going to be receiving five that still had vital signs.

Calls were made to various departments and soon there were several Respiratory Therapists briskly walking down our corridor with ventilators in tow. Several folks came up from the OR to aid in intubations should our Docs have difficulty with the burned airways.

One by one the patients arrived and soon the ER was a buzz with the rapid influx.

Four of the burn patients were intubated and they were covered in soot. The sight of black ash in their nostrils bore witness to the hell they'd been immersed in.

Reaching down to pull a scrap of clothing from under one lady I was horrified to see a large slab of skin slough off onto the shirt. It was as if she'd been boiled alive. Well, I guess she had been.

These folks were all elderly, and it was just too much of a shock to their system. One by one they succumbed to their injuries. There was nothing we could do.

The following day our department received a commendation from the hospital. Job well done. Sure didn't feel like a job well done. A loss of five out of five is a terrible record.

Intellectually I knew that there was always very little chance we could have saved them. As a fellow human it really sucked, for the sight of their burned bodies and melted skin stayed with me a long time. I made the mistake of letting my mind drift and I thought, "To have lived so long, to have seen so much history, and then to die this way." It was just terrible.

Something was beginning to happen inside of me. There was a hardness starting to form. It was hard yet hollow. Empty. I was beginning to feel the first effects of something I could not classify. In fact, I wasn't really aware it was anything significant.

Only years later would I realize that my heart was beginning to harden.

White Foam

A young man came in who'd opened a bottle of liquid rat poison, lifted it to his lips and chugged the entire contents in one swift gulp.

The chemical reaction within his body began swiftly and in a matter of seconds became catastrophic. When he first entered through our doors via ambulance stretcher, I thought it odd that he was not taken into the main Resuscitation Room but was moved to a private room.

I soon learned the wisdom of this decision.

White foam poured from his mouth and as fast as I suctioned this froth it instantly was replaced by more. If I had not witnessed this continuous flow, I'd have not believed the human body capable of creating it. I tried not to think about what his lungs must have looked like. He was drowning.

Convulsing caused foam to eject from his mouth. Thankfully we wore impervious blue plastic gowns, shoe covers, and face shields which protected our skin. Flecks of foam slid down my visor. I tried not to over think the situation. Just do what needs to be done. The poor guy's immediate problem was his airway, so I kept an eye on the suction canister, ready to change it when it filled.

We were prepping to get him intubated when the Medical Director of the Emergency Department poked his head in and yelled, "Everyone! Drop what you're doing! Out! Everyone out now!"

We stood there for a second, trying to comprehend the order we'd just been given. The doctor was quite forceful this time, "You heard me, get the Hell out of there right now! All of you! Leave him!"

We stepped out into the hallway and the doctor gave us our orders, "Listen, this is a very dangerous situation. Every ounce of foam coming out of his mouth is toxic. There's nothing we can do for him. He's not going to survive this."

I took a deep breath and looked at the dried flecks of foam on the outside of my visor. This was real.

The doctor continued, "All of you will go to your locker rooms, take showers and rinse off for several minutes. Toss your scrubs on the floor and never touch them again. You can consider them gone. They will be collected in hazardous material bags and properly discarded."

Good grief!

He continued, "We'll get you replacement scrubs from the OR. For now, go to the shower immediately."

So, we quick stepped to the showers with the vision of white foam pouring out of this young man's mouth.

Lathering up with soap and watching it swirl into the drain I couldn't help but see that foam pouring out of this guy's mouth and nose. Horrific.

I slumped my head down and let the warm water run down my head and cascade to the tile floor. My eyes were closed tight but my thoughts were on this young man who surely could not have imagined such a horrible death.

How could things get so bad? Why would anyone get to a point that death seemed a better choice? Were such people just weak? I didn't know or understand the decision to take one's own life.

In time to come I'd be able to identify more and more with this young man. I would see just how dark things can get and that no, weakness or strength had nothing to do with a decision of such magnitude. There were many other more complex workings at play. Very soon I would discover this in my own reality.

The Jedi

One of my buddies in the ER is Chris Esparza, an RN. Now, I'm a huge Star Wars fan but I'm a rookie compared to Chris. We both were kids when the Star Wars movies began rolling out in the late 70s and early 80s.

For Halloween in first grade, I was R2D2 and in second I was a Storm Trooper. That was 1981 thus making me a charter member of the Star Wars fan club.

Fast forward twenty-five years and I'm working in the Trauma Center alongside Chris. One night shift we were tending to a lady who was in her late nineties. The back of her stretcher was straight up because of the hunch in her back. Chris was on one side of the stretcher and I on the other.

I was fidgeting with the monitor leads while Chris tended to the tape of the IV he'd just started.

This lady would not sit still. We were trying to be patient but for crying out loud. Lady, can you please hold still for at least thirty seconds, that's all I need. Of course, I didn't say that, but I sure did think it.

"Ma'am try and hold still while we get you on the monitor and secure this IV," was the best I could do.

She seemed to ignore me. I looked over at Chris who just shook his head and smiled.

The lady began to fidget with the blankets around her waist, pulling here and pushing there, desperately searching for something. She had this look of concern that told us something very important seemed to be missing.

Chris gently put his hand on her right shoulder, bent down to her field of vision and kindly asked, "Ma'am, what's wrong? Are you missing something? Do you need some help?"

The lady had her head turned toward me on her left and was in a bowing position when she said, "I can't find my glasses."

Suddenly her eyeglasses dropped off the right side of her head. As the glasses fell to her right, she was looking left. In one motion she lifted her right hand up off the bed and caught the glasses in midair.

When she caught them, and while still looking to the left, she said, "Oh there they are" and when she finished saying the word "are" she turned her head all the way to the right and then down at the glasses resting safely in her right hand.

Chris and I instantly locked eyes, and with mirrored looks of astonishment simultaneously exclaimed, "JEDI!"

A Visit from Spider Man

It was Halloween and the night was dragging.

One of the nurses called out, "Dennis, you have visitors in the front."

"Who could that be?" I thought.

Pushing open the doors to triage I instantly saw my nephew Seth who was about five years old and dressed up like Buzz Lightyear. My niece Alexis was a princess and looked adorable.

They were not the only ones dressed up.

From the crowd of waiting patients came an old creaky voice, "Hey Spidey! What-cha doing here?"

I turned and there was my dad in full Hollywood quality Spider Man costume. He was bent down in a crouching Spidey pose with legs spread apart in an action pose, with the wrist bent out like he was shooting webs.

My dad answered the lady, "I was swinging between buildings and fell. Need to get my back checked out."

Everyone was laughing. It was a huge morale booster for those waiting for their turn to be called.

Well, let me clarify, not everyone was laughing. I was mortified.

"Dad!" I called out. "Come with me!"

Spiderman waved to those in the waiting room, spreading some cheer and called out, "Hope you all get to feeling better."

I took dad into the Family Waiting Room and said, "Dad, it's obvious you're not aware of this but that costume is so tight it looks like you're smuggling olives."

My mom burst out laughing. Tears were in her eyes because she knew exactly what I was referring to.

My dad, slid his mask off and said, "What? What do you mean 'smuggling olives?"

Of course, that made mom laugh even harder.

I pointed down at his groin.

He looked and immediately turned as red as his costume and cried out, "Oh crap!"

Oh my gosh we laughed until we cried. Even all these years later we still talk about the great Spider Man Smuggling Olives caper.

Emergency Fast Food

I recall working triage one day when a young lady ran up to the desk breathless and exclaimed, "I need help with my grandpa! He's out in the car and not acting right!"

I grabbed some gloves and went out to the "Patient Drop-Off" area.

Approaching the vehicle, I could see an older Hispanic male sitting in the rear passenger compartment with his left arm up on the back of the seat. His head was flopped backward, and his mouth agape.

I opened the passenger door and shouted, "Hello sir! Hello Sir! How are you doing!"

While I shouted, I rubbed his chest with my knuckles, applying pressure to his sternum. I reached up to his neck and felt no pulse. When I tried to pull him out to begin CPR, I noticed an unopened McDonalds bag between his legs.

As I was pulling him out the door I testily asked, "Did you guys stop for food on the way here?"

The same young girl, with tears in her eyes answered, almost as a remorseful confession, "Yeah, we were hungry, so we stopped and got everyone some food."

I glared up at her and began chest compressions while others ran to get a stretcher. I asked, "Who is this man to you?"

Between sobs she replied, "He's my grandfather."

I nodded my head and asked, "What kind of complaints did he have today?"

The distraught weeping young lady coughs and between heaving breaths says, "Well, all day he's been complaining about chest pains, but he always has those, so we figured it was nothing too…"

Before she can finish the sentence, she buried her face in her hands.

It's a terrible end to a story that any other day would have played out exactly as she planned. I felt sorry for her. Later, after we turned the monitors off, unplugged the ventilator and cleaned him up a bit, I walked her into the room so she could sit with him a while. Make her peace.

I handed her a box of tissues and said, "Look, it's not your fault that your grandpa died. He had a long history of cardiac issues. It wasn't the prolonged trip to the ER that killed him, it was his forty-five years of smoking and not taking his medications."

She nodded her head but said nothing. I stepped out to give her and the family some privacy. I then returned to triage where the blood draw requests were stacking up. The critical task was to start working on this growing list of blood draws I needed to do, for our triage patients who were restless and angry.

At our core we humans are selfish however, I know that if people in the waiting room knew what I was doing for this family they would have understood the prolonged time.

Their reality was waiting and waiting, for what?

My reality was consoling a family who'd just lost a loved one and because of the circumstances they felt guilty about it. I was sweating from doing CPR and friggin bummed out that this guy had died. So, when I returned to the blood draw station and called the first patient, I pretended to just carry on like everything was normal. Stiff upper lip. Smile. Do your job Dennis.

Was everything fine with me? I mean, it's not like this was the first person I'd seen die. Something about innocently stopping for fast food, the awful twist of fate, and the guilt of that fateful decision haunting this family really bothered me. I wanted to make it right for them by getting him back.

Truth was that we had no time to deliberate about such things. No time to discuss this event with my coworkers and talk through the situation. Nothing. Our waiting room was full, and our triage nurses were even then taking EMS reports from inbound Ambulance and Helicopter patients. Keep working. Feel later.

This man and that bag of McDonalds between his legs was obviously seared into my brain. What was I supposed to do with this vision? Well, with the absence of advice or mental checks by those in leadership I did what I thought everyone else was doing. I shoved it deep down into a secret chamber in my heart. It was a dark place and the existence of this chamber scared me. I was too afraid to investigate it and too proud to talk of its existence. I pressed on.

He'll Be Back

Oh, it was a cold miserable rainy night (So many great stories start that way don't they). The wind was out of the north causing the temps to hover around the low 40s. Cold for San Antonio.

We had a teenage boy who said he wanted to kill himself, so the Police brought him in for evaluation and counseling.

This kid was a punk. He cussed out the nurses and would not answer any of the questions the doctor asked him. We'd managed to get him into a patient gown, and we seemed to be making headway until he found out he couldn't go out for a cigarette.

He demanded, "Let me out so I can get a cigarette!"

One of the nurses said, "I'm sorry young man but this is a nonsmoking facility, and even if it wasn't you are not of an age that we can allow you to smoke."

The boy dropped an "F" Bomb, heckled his mother, and then took off running down the hall.

I went chasing after him and was gaining. If he went straight, he would emerge into the waiting room where our Security had a desk, and they'd stop him.

He turned left.

I was a few feet behind him when he slammed against the Ambulance Bay doors causing them to fly open. Out the door he sprinted, out into the dark of night and into a world of northerly winds, pelting ice cold rain and little hope for warmth or shelter.

When he pushed through the door and took off outside, we all hit the brakes and let him go.

Someone said, "Aren't you gonna go get him?"

My answer, "Nope. That's what the police are for. Besides its too cold. He'll be back."

About twenty minutes later the nurses in triage heard a knocking on the Ambulance Bay doors. There was our stray cat, shaking, soaked to the bone and incredibly repentant.

We brought him inside, took him to the restroom where he could dry off and put on a fresh gown and warm socks.

Once he emerged, we had two piping hot blankets for him, fresh from the warmer.

Nothing was said about his excursion out into the wild. Words were not needed for the elements had taught him plenty.

Rescue Mission…Wait…What?

It was my day off and I was enjoying every second of it. My cell phone rang. I was tempted to ignore it but I looked at the screen and saw it was a good friend of mine who's a sister to me. I answered.

She got right to it, "Dennis, hey you know there's an ENA[47] Conference in town, right?"

I laughed, "Yeah, I'm aware. Why? Oh god, what's up?"

She didn't laugh but rather began giving me instructions, "Hey I need you to swing by the ER. Call Carl[48] when you're pulling up to the Ambulance Bay. He's going to walk up to your window and hand you a brown bag of IV supplies. We have a bunch of nurses here puking their guts out. We've been partying pretty hard."

I replied, "Ok, will do."

She texted me the address and room number of the hotel where they were all staying. I did exactly as instructed.

---

[47] Emergency Nurses Association
[48] A Pseudonym

I pulled up to the ER, texted Carl who quickly emerged with a large brown bag containing IV tubing, fluids, IV catheters and nausea medication. I don't think I even braked. I just coasted by. Nothing was said. It was kind of naughty, but it was an important mission.

Downtown I found the appropriate hotel, parked, and made my way up. Two knocks and the door opened to reveal a couple nurses lying passed out on both beds. On the other side of the room two RNs tended to one of their own puking into a trash can.

My friend grabbed the bag from me and said, "Good job Blocker."

I smiled and said, "Are you guys ok to start IV's or do you need me to. My hand is probably a lot steadier than yours."

I was assured they were fine, but I hung out just to make sure. I found a lone high back chair against a wall and sat by like the sheepdog overwatching his flock.

Within a few minutes IV bags were hanging from nails that once held framed pictures. Drip, drip, drip, went the IV fluids and then the Zofran was administered.

Soon the beds held quiet, resting frontline veterans. I wondered if they had been successful in drowning the demons that haunted them. I was glad they had each other to lean on. It's hard to relate to those with no clue of the horrors we see daily. This time of revelry was important for these life savers.

I stood, hugged my friend, "Let me know if you need anything else. You guys be careful."

She smiled, "We will and thank you so much."

With that I was out the door, in my car and on my way back to my house to continue watching my movie. One eye on the movie and the other on my cell phone.

Long Blonde Hair

EMS came rushing into the trauma room with a new patient. They were running. Never a good sign for EMS runs nowhere.

One of the paramedics began to yell out the report, "We have a ten-year-old female who was checking on her neighbor's dog who seemed to be in distress. The dog was hung up on a fence by its collar. This girl knew the animal, had grown up with him and tried to free him. When she pulled on the collar the dog caught her by the throat and clamped down. Neighbors were bashing the dog over the head with shovels, but it would not release her. Police had to shoot him. By then she was unresponsive."

There was nothing to be done. Arteries and veins were intact. Her organs unmolested. The dog had crushed her airway. There was nothing we could do. She was dead before she arrived.

About thirty minutes later I wheeled her into a private room so her family could come view her body. I took an examination light, flipped it on and turned the beam to the ceiling. I positioned chairs around the bed with boxes of tissue. I placed a pillow under her head. Then the nurse and I fixed the blanket and sheets to make it look like she was just tucked in to go to sleep. We brushed her beautiful long blonde hair and lay it gently along her meek shoulders.

This scene would often play over and over in my nightmares. Even twenty years later she would visit me in my dreams. I see her standing in a beam of light, surrounded by thick oily darkness. She is silent. Unblinking. Perfectly still. Her eyes fixed on me. On her neck, the bite wounds from the dog.[49]

---

[49] I truly believe her reemergence into my dreams was caused by the fact that my daughter Lauren would grow up to have long blonde hair and she looks very similar.

Angels and Demons

As our department had a Psych wing we saw our fair share of people with some serious mental issues. These patients needed medical clearance before they'd be accepted for a psychiatry evaluation. This meant that our ER saw an incredible number of these patients.

The majority of psychiatry patients were there because they made a statement to family or the Police that they wanted to kill themselves. Such a proclamation earned an immediate "Emergency Detention" by a law enforcement entity. Meaning, they could not leave the facility until discharged by the Psych Department. Basically, they were gonna get help whether they liked it or not.

90% of these patients were not a danger to anyone but themselves. However, that last ten percent were extremely dangerous.

The scariest thing about that ten percent was that they often exhibited no outward display of aggression or anger. Sitting in a chair, they seemed to be oblivious to those around them. Staring straight forward, blinking, listening to the voice (or voices) in their head. They seemed to epitomize a pressure cooker. Who knew when they'd blow?

You had to develop survival skills in that environment. Never turn your back. Make sure such a patient is never between you and the only exit from a room. Never wear ID lanyards around your neck because they can be used to choke you to death. You know, rules like that.

I recall helping to take care of a psych patient who was guarded by a Texas Ranger. The dude's eyes were bugged out of his head and his hair looked like he'd been a conduit of electricity.

Seeing one of our own policemen walk by I asked him, "What's a guy have to do to rate a Texas Ranger as a guard? I've never seen a Ranger before."

The officer replied, "Well this particular dude rolled up to a Border Patrol checkpoint and refused to answer questions posed to him by the Federal agents. Alarmed by his erratic behavior the agents demanded he exit the vehicle so they could search the trunk."

As the officer tells the story I glance over at the prisoner who stares straight ahead. Unblinking.

Continuing with the details the officer says, "The guy walked to the rear of the vehicle, placed the key into the receptacle and turned it. There was a slight 'click' sound as the release mechanism was engaged. The trunk began to rise and as it did the squirrely driver pulled a knife from his pants and began to savagely slash his own wrist."

Sure enough, I looked over at the guy and his wrist was wrapped tightly with a bloody bandage.

The officer wasn't finished with the story though, "The agents tackled the guy and took the knife from him. First-aid was administered. One of the other agents peered into the trunk and saw the body of a young lady who would turn out to be the guy's girlfriend. Creepy thing is that after some investigation the agents discovered something troubling. When the dude left his home state out East, he had his girlfriend and her sister in the car. They still can't find the younger sister. They think he may have killed her and dumped her body along one of those rural roads in the hill country."

Such horrific stories were commonplace. We saw the worst of the worst psych cases, and these would sometimes prove deadly.

One night shift I had an orientee with me and we were assigned to triage. Suddenly we heard cursing and yelling coming from one of our treatment rooms.

I said, "Let's go!"

We sprinted down the hall, turned the corner just when an examination light came toppling out and crashed to the ground, shattering the lens.

When I turned to enter the room, I could see a San Antonio Police officer and a Bexar County Sheriff wrestling with a patient on the floor.

"Ahhhh!"

The patient had a mouthful of the Police officer's thigh and was biting down as hard as he could. The female deputy was trying to get the guy's right arm behind his back so she could cuff him, but he thumped her over the head and was reaching around her back.

The deputy couldn't see it, but the assailant had his hand on the grip of her pistol and was tugging on it, trying to remove it from the holster. My orientee and I glanced at each other and in that split second of silence so much was said, "If we don't step in people are going to die. These officers are losing."

After a short but raucous tussle we got control of this dude while others tended to the injuries of the officer and deputy. It had been a close call.

This was not an anomaly. We had nurses and medics disarm patients many times. I recall two of our nurses pulled a linen sheet off a patient and saw a handgun in the guy's lap. They instantly snatched it up, ran out of the room and called for the hospital police.

Do you recall what I said about Alpha Nurses? Well, they're vital. They saw danger and instantly acted. It would've been easy to just run out of the room. In fact, it would have been preferable for them do so and let the police handle the firearm situation. The "it" factor in these nurses made them grab the gun. It was in them to do so.

Now, of course I'm not saying that nurses should become the warriors of the hospital. However, there is that breed of people who see a situation and act. It's their character, their very core of who they are and thank God for them.

Of the hundreds of psych patients I helped take care of there were many who claimed to be "the devil." Some didn't claim anything, they just acted like demon possessed people they'd seen in the movies. These folks were putting on a show and we all knew it.

However, there were a handful that creeped me out and made the hair on the back of my neck standup.

One night shift I heard cursing, yelling and heavy thumping sounds coming from a closed room.

I asked one of the nurses, "What's going on in there?"

She replied, "Oh, they're trying to restrain this combative guy."

"Sounds like they need some help," was my reply.

I opened the door, stepped in and when I did the guy who was in mortal combat with the police suddenly relaxed and lay still on the gurney. The police and security personnel began to restrain him. As they worked the patient never took his gaze off me. Our eyes were fixed on each other.

This guy smiled a wide Cheshire cat grin, ear to ear. The eyes communicated something dark and sinister yet perceptive. The room seemed permeated with a heavy oppressive atmosphere. It was suddenly as if we were the only two people in the room. With a hushed tone I calmly asked, "You know, don't you?"

He didn't speak, he never stopped grinning nor did his eyes turn away from mine. He simply and slowly nodded his head up and down in acknowledgement of my statement.

When I said, "You know, don't you?" I was referring to the fact that I'm a Christian. He confirmed my suspicion. That heavy presence in the room and the wicked grin made my blood run cold.

I turned and walked out.

Let me say this about such patients. There is no classification in the hospital chart for "Demon Possession." He was going to be medically cleared and then sent to the psych department where he would get a script for meds that would hide his real problem.

Let me be clear. I'm no zealot. I never stood on a table, held a Bible in my hand, extended a raised fist toward the heavens and cried out, "Be gone DEVIL!"

Heck no! I knew enough about possession to know that handling those situations required someone who was both physically and spiritually prepared. I was just a dude who happened to walk in on an entity who recognized who I represented. It was a spiritual standoff and then a stand down so to speak. Which I was grateful for.[50]

---

[50] I have two more such stories, but they can only be told around a campfire. They're too creepy and I'm not interested in giving such unseen forces that much publicity.

On another shift a buddy came up to me and said, "Hey Blocker, they want you to go to bed twelve, there's someone there claiming to be the Devil."

I was perplexed, "Why do I have to go? I don't want to meet the Devil."

The guy laughed and said, "Well, you're a Christian and all that stuff. They think you'll handle this better."

I just shook my head and thought, "Crud."

Before I entered the room, I took my badge and stuck it in my pocket. I wanted to try something.

Walking into the room I noticed that the "Devil" was actually a female prisoner of the County Jail. She wore the requisite orange jump suit, gray socks, and orange flipflops. Her wrists were handcuffed as were her ankles.

At the foot of the stretcher, perusing a magazine, sat a Sheriff Deputy who I knew. He smiled, rolled his eyes, and jerked his head toward the prisoner.

I smiled. Oh boy, this is gonna be good.

The inmate was staring at a space between her feet. Her eyes were bugged out and she was rocking back and forth.

All the while she was repeating the phrase, "I'm the Devil. I'm the Devil. I'm the Devil."

I approached her gurney and sat on a chair to her right. She ignored me but kept rocking and repeating that phrase over and over and over.

I could feel the eyes of my buddies behind me, and I wondered what they were thinking. I pressed on.

After taking a deep breath I said, "Hello ma'am. I understand you are the Devil."

No visible acknowledgement that I had spoken to her. Just the continuous phrase, "I'm the Devil, I'm the Devil. I'm the Devil."

I looked over at the deputy who was smiling but looking down at the magazine. I'm sure he could sense I was looking at him. I was telepathically sending him the message, "What the heck did you bring us tonight?"

I turned back to, well, the Devil and said, "Ma'am, if you're the Devil you'll be able to tell me what my name is."

She suddenly froze in place. Staring straight ahead at the wall. Was it me or did the room suddenly get eerily quiet? It seemed as if the oxygen had been sucked out of the room. The deputy froze, he had not expected me to say this and had accordingly lost his smile.

Would she respond?

A few awkward seconds of silence elapsed, and the woman's face broke into a huge grin, she laughed, turned toward me, and said, "You got me!"

We all laughed as did the inmate. The deputy rose out of his seat, holding his gut, laughing.

I walked out into the hallway. My buddies were talking over each other, "That was amazing Blocker!" "How did you know to ask that?" "Friggin awesome dude!"

One of my coworkers said, "No, seriously, how did you know to say that?"

I replied, "I knew she was a fake because the Devil doesn't advertise who he is. He's called the Angel of Light because he traps folks. He isn't trying to scare off anybody."

Then someone asked, "Yeah, well, how cool would that have been if suddenly she looked at you and said, 'Your name is Dennis Blocker and I saw you when...'"

Everyone burst into laughter, and I replied, "Well, in that case you would've seen me running."

There is evil and there is good. Yin and Yang.

On a separate occasion one of our doctors approached and said, "Hey Dennis, can you please go into the Trauma Room and stay with a family. They're waiting for their pastor to arrive."

I had questions of course. For example, "What am I stepping into?"

Turns out the lady had been shot in the head by her husband. The scum bag then shot their five-year-old son and then turned the gun on himself and pulled the trigger.

If the story were not sad enough the lady was three months pregnant. We all knew that once the mothers heart stopped beating, the unborn child would die shortly thereafter. There was nothing we could do about it.

The Doc said, "Dennis, I just want you to be there with the family. They're waiting for their pastor to arrive and then they've decided to let her go."

I replied, "Oh, so they want to turn everything off? The ventilators, medication drips etc."

The Doc nodded his head and then walked me over to the room.

We entered and after I was introduced to the family the doctor left to go tend to other patients.

I said very little. I mean, what do you say? This was the worst day of their life. No parent wants to bury their child and how much worse to bury your child and grandchild. It was numbing to contemplate.

In the room, sitting in a chair holding the young lady's left hand was her mother. Continuously she rubbed her hand, kissed it, and caressed her arm, "We love you baby girl. Your mom and dad are here with you. Your brother is here and so is grandma."

I fought hard to maintain my composure. I refused to show emotion and it was tough. I just forced my brain to think about other things, the tasks I had to do, the upcoming movie releases, anything to keep me from going, "there."

Behind the mother stood dad, who massaged his wife's shoulders while tears slowly coursed down his cheeks. At the foot of the bed, also sitting in a chair, was grandma who massaged the feet and rubbed her granddaughter's calves.

To the right, sitting in a chair was the brother who held his sister's right hand and quietly cried.

Witnessing the scene was hard, incredibly hard.

The monitor would alarm every now and then because the young lady, though technically alive, was having one catastrophic event after another take place in her body and brain.

She had vital signs, but they were of course at the extremes. Systolic blood pressure over 250 and a heart rate that was well over 150. Her body was refusing to quit. She had a strong spirit.

It seemed like an eternity, but the pastor finally did arrive. He shook hands all around and hugged everyone. I liked him immediately. Had a nice vibe about him. He was no tele-evangelist; this pastor was a man who cared about his folks.

The preacher said, "Ok, let's all join hands."

The mother, father, grandma, pastor, brother, and our patient all held hands.

The pastor prayed, "Dear Lord, we don't know why these things happen. This is a senseless act that we are finding hard to reconcile. We thank you for her. She was a wonderful mother, a wonderful daughter, granddaughter and sister."

He paused, took a deep breath and continued, "Lord, the family has asked me, to ask you, if you would please just take her right now. They don't want her to suffer. In Jesus name we pray. Amen."

At that very moment the monitor flatlined. She was gone that very instant.

Stunned, I reached over and felt for a pulse. There was none. I looked over at the pastor and said, "Sir, she's gone."

I was dumb struck. If I had not seen it with my own eyes, I'd not have believed it.

I imagined two angels standing at attention beside the gurney. Once the pastor asked for God to take them, permission was granted. One angel reached down for the momma and the other for the baby. Off they went.

I'll never forget it.

The Veterans

San Antonio is called "Military City, USA" for there are currently three active military bases here but for decades there were five.[51] With all these bases around the city there is of course a corresponding large population of retired military and veterans who've made San Antonio their home.

I've had the privilege of taking care of many of these men and women.

One day in the Medical Resuscitation room[52], which we called "Med Resus", I took care of a gentleman who needed to get transferred over to the VA Hospital.

Our facility was connected to the VA by a skywalk. At lunch time their employees would go to our cafeteria and our employees would go to theirs. It seems variety was the all-important factor.

Anyway, this fella needed to get over to an ICU bed, but they were delaying transfer because they didn't have any

---

[51] Lackland AFB (still active), Kelly AFB (decommissioned), Brooks AFB (decommissioned), Randolph AFB (still active) and Fort Sam Houston (still active)

[52] There are two areas for the most critical patients. They were divided up by those involving trauma and those suffering from a medical condition.

room. Or so one of the employees we spoke with reported. However, we knew from a previous conversation with their bed placement team that they did in fact have the room.

I was updating the gentleman on the fact that we were still waiting on a bed for him. Suddenly a thought crossed my mind and I asked, "Sir, what did you do during WWII?"

He replied, "Oh, I was in the infantry, you know, a foot soldier."

I smiled and said, "Yes, I do know all about you fellas. I love WWII history and have read tons of books on the subject."

He was beaming.

I went on, "Sir, were you in Europe or the Pacific? Did you see combat?"

He calmy answered, "Well I was in Europe and yes, I saw quite a bit of combat. I was in the invasion of Normandy, D-Day."

I was stunned. I'd never talked with anyone who'd been there.

I pressed on, "What beach did you hit and in what wave did you go in?"

He grew serious, looked me dead on and said, "I went in on Omaha beach, first wave."[53]

Incredible.

Before my brain could catch up my mouth asked, "How did you survive sir?"

He laughed and said, "Well, you can probably guess that I was hit. I mean, you didn't come away from that beach unharmed. It was just luck of the draw that I survived."

This old warrior turned his head and added, "Almost all of the men I went in with died."

I patted his hand with mine and said, "Sir, it's an honor to meet you. Thank you for what you did for us."

The words seemed hollow, insignificant to the magnitude of what he had endured for our freedom.

---

[53] If you have seen the movie *Saving Private Ryan* well then you will know that opening scene was Omaha Beach, first wave.

I made my way over to the PA who was working hard to get this man a bed across the street.

Stepping up beside him I said, "Hey man, that guy you're trying to get a bed for at the VA, well he was at Omaha Beach, D-Day, First Wave, wounded in action."

I didn't wait for an answer, I stepped away as he picked up the phone and called bed placement.

Someone picked up on their end and I heard our PA very clearly say, "So, this guy we're trying to get a bed for in your hospital, well he was at Omaha Beach, D-Day invasion, first wave. Are you seriously gonna tell me you don't have a bed for him?"

A few more seconds of silence as he listened and then he said, "Ok, thank you."

He looked over at me, grinned and said, "They're assigning him a bed right now."

We both laughed with delight. Our hero would be comfortable tonight.

You know, some of these fellas would just come through and I'd have to pry it out of them. My first clue would be their birth year. If I saw 1918, 1921, 1925 well then, I knew they were prime candidates to have served in the war.

Sometimes though I'd get some shocking replies to my query.

One night shift I was hooking up an elderly lady to a blood pressure machine. I glanced down at her wrist band and saw her birthyear.

I asked, "Ma'am what were you doing during World War II. I see the year you were born so you would've been a teenager during that time."

She answered in English with a beautiful accent, "Well, actually I remember it quite well. I was born and raised in Belgium. One day I was helping my father tend our little garden. I heard a terrible droning in the air. I looked up and the sky was full of German planes. We had just been invaded by Germany. We were at war."

One lady that I took care of had her registration number tattooed to her forearm. She was a Jew who had survived a concentration camp and had made her way to America after the war.

One fella said, "Yes, I was in the Navy during the war."

He told me the ship, and I immediately went to the computer, opened up my ancestry.com account, typed in the fella's birthday and name then printed out some Documents.

Walking over to the fella I handed him a stack of papers and said, "Here are some muster rolls from your ship. I see your name on there. I also included and Action Report from your time at Okinawa."

He could not believe it. He had tears of joy in his eyes. He went down the list of names and spouted out, "Yeah, this guy was in the Engine Room, a real clown!"

On and on he went down the list remembering old shipmates. He seemed to get better right in front of our eyes. His wife couldn't believe the transformation. I brought a laptop over to him and showed him some pictures that were online.

"Hey that's me! Right there!" he shouted.

More people gathered round and listened as he told about the picture of him loading troops into his amphibious craft called an LCVP. What a time. What a memory.

One fella I met was a fighter pilot in the famous Tuskegee Airmen. Actually, through the years I've met two of these pilots in the hospitals I worked at. How cool is that!

It was such a privilege to take care of these men and women. To show my esteem for them I would ask each of them their rank. Then, the rest of the shift, I would address them as such.

"Sergeant Gomez, sir I need to take you over to CT for a quick scan Sarge."

"Colonel Smith, I need to check your blood sugar sir, see where you're at."

When it was time for me to clock out for the day I'd stand at the door and say, "Sir/Ma'am, my shift is over. I'm heading home. You take care and get better."

With that, I'd stand ramrod straight and pop a sharp salute. They'd smile, return the salute.

I know I was not supposed to show favoritism to any of my patients, but the veterans just had a special place in my heart. Many of them had been ravaged by decades of nightmares and as such some had never achieved their full potential.

I made it my mission to be sure each veteran that I contacted knew he/she was appreciated. In the large scheme of things, it didn't make a bit of difference to their life, but perhaps the respect I showed might have rekindled that pride.

These folks had answered the call when their country was in need. They had it in them to do great things. Sometimes they just needed to be reminded. Perhaps standing in the door, saluting and saying, "Good night Sargent Gomez. I'm heading home now," would remind them of how friggin awesome they really were. At the very least, they knew I appreciated them and recognized their rank and service. I owed them that. Heck, we all do.

They All Run Together

I witnessed so much pain and suffering that after a while the really horrible cases just started to blur from memory. There was just too many to remember. Of course, that's a good thing too for who wants to remember all that crud.

I recall how horrified I was when a friend asked about a child abuse case they heard about. I was terrified that I'd forgotten all about this kiddo. Only two days had elapsed since I'd taken care of the toddler and I'd already forgotten about him.

Was this a self-preservation mechanism or was my mind just incapable of storing any more horrendous details? I didn't know but the fact that I could so easily dismiss such a horrific crime really bothered me.

That's the way it was in the Level One Trauma Center. Intense. Brutal. Unforgiving. Relentless. Exhausting. Every once in a while, the universe would throw you a "good save" but even that was cruel. It would reinvigorate and keep us pushing forward, skipping lunches, skipping restroom breaks. Fatigue. Anguish.

Night shift and night shift.

Now I have sudden, sporadic triggers that will dust off the old data banks and flash morbid scenes onto my mind's eye. Whether I like it or not.

For example, there was the infant who was flown to our helipad with CPR in progress. It was the first time I'd seen the aircrew ditch any semblance of decorum. "F" bombs were dropped before the report was given.

It went something like this, "F#$%ing family was more interested in the championship game on the television than in the CPR we were doing on their baby!"

One of the Trauma Nurses thought she heard wrong, so she said, "Excuse me, did you just say the family was watching a game while you were doing CPR?"

The flight nurse disgustedly replied, "Yeah, they were cheering and hollering while we were resuscitating their baby."

We were enraged but shelved that for future processing.

I removed the diaper and was horrified to see that it contained actual layers of poop. You can't make this up. I'm telling you that there was an actual timeline of bowel movements in the diaper. As you can imagine the baby's bottom was full of sores.

Turns out the baby had been crying so the parents closed the door so they could watch the game.[54]

Meanwhile the baby managed to crawl up over the rail and slide over. Unfortunately, the t-shirt caught on a rail of the bed frame, and it hung beside the bed and suffocated. We were unable to revive this poor little one.

I recall one teenaged gang banger who'd been stabbed in his left upper clavicle. He was combative, pale, and sweating like crazy. All signs pointed to a young man who had minutes, maybe even seconds, to live.

He was swinging at us, desperate to survive. He could feel the darkness closing in on him and he wasn't ready to go. He looked over at me with a desperate, caged animal expression and screamed, "I don't want to die bro! Don't let me die!"

I was trying to hold him down so we could start an IV and get some blood into him. This was no time for sweet talk, so I exclaimed, "You're going to die bro if you don't quit fighting us! Let us help you!"

---

[54] It never dawned on them that the baby might stop crying if they would change the diaper and heal up those sores.

Suddenly his eyes rolled back in his head, he slumped back and promptly flatlined.[55] The trauma resident looked at the Attending who ordered, "Cut him!"

The Resident Doctor took a 21-blade scalpel and made a long incision to the left side of his chest, following the contours of the rib cage. The incision was professional, deep, and incredibly fast.

Suddenly the teenager sat up, screamed, "Ahhhhhhhhhhhh!" and grabbed the left side of his chest.

I can tell you that the oxygen was sucked out of that room. Somewhere in the back someone dropped a stoic F-Bomb.

The horrified Resident looked over at the Attending and half-cried, "You said cut him!"

The faculty surgeon smiled, calmly nodded his head, and matter-of-factly said, "Package him up, let's go to the OR."

Turns out the procedure was exactly what the kid needed. A lacerated artery in the clavicle had been filling the chest with blood causing the lung and then the heart to

---

[55] His heart rhythm on the monitor was now a straight line. No beats.

be compressed.[56] The scalpel incision caused the blood to rapidly evacuate the chest cavity, allowing this young man's heart to go right on beating.

The kid made a full (yet lengthy) recovery and hopefully took advantage of his second chance at life.

Not everyone got second chances though. Some situations you just wouldn't believe if you had not seen it. I recall we were working on a guy who'd taken a shotgun blast to the chest. He was in cardiac arrest, well, more accurately he suffered a traumatic arrest as a result of trauma sustained to his chest.

Anyway, the guy lost his pulse within seconds of EMS placing him on our stretcher. I was busy setting up the Level One Rapid Infuser in anticipation of infusing the blood we'd called for.

The obvious problem was that pellets from the shotgun had penetrated vital blood vessels in his chest cavity. He was leaking blood into his chest and not circulating it through his body.

---

[56] Cardiac tamponade is the accumulation of fluid around the heart muscle, which places excessive pressure on this organ.

The Trauma Attending conducted, what in trauma trench parlance is called a "Clam Shell" thoracotomy. The surgeon needed to see the respiratory and circulatory organs, and close any traumatic holes he found in the vessels, heart, and lungs with sutures.

Now this "Clam Shell" meant the Attending would make an incision across the guy's chest from left to right. The incision would be full thickness, through all the layers of skin. The surgeon would then reveal the sternum bone and taking a chisel and hammer split the sternum allowing him to "pop the hood."

I'm sure you can imagine what that refers to. If not, imagine the rib cage is lifted up like the hood of a car.

Well, I had seen this done many times by this point so that was not such a big deal. The odd thing that made this situation stand out was what happened after the surgeon had the heart started again.

We were quickly prepping the patient and stretcher for the transport to OR. As such I was helping the nurses sort the IV pumps and units of blood hanging from IV poles.[57] It always seemed a pump was left plugged in when we started to walk with the patient. Not this time, I would head

---

[57] This literally happened in seconds.

those little electric cord gnomes off. I personally unplugged each pump from the wall and quickly rolled up the cords. Mere seconds had elapsed.

Next, I needed to be sure the oxygen tank under the stretcher was good. So, I bent down to check the oxygen level. I was down at the right-hand side of the patient, kneeling looking at the tank to see the gauge when I heard a familiar voice ask a question.

"How are we on oxygen," asked someone.

I looked up and noticed it was the Respiratory Therapist who was manually ventilating our patient with an Ambu bag.

I answered, "We're good brother. The tank's full. If you unplug the bag from the wall, I'll put you on the O's[58] under here."

Nothing unusual about that casual, nonplused conversation. Except that the entire conversation took place through the gaping six-inch circular shotgun blast in this guy's chest.

---

[58] EMS and ER slang for the word "oxygen."

Later I walked up to RT and said, "You do realize we had a casual conversation about oxygen through this poor guy's shotgun blast."

We both laughed. It was surreal.

It's amazing how hardened one gets after extensive exposure to such sights.

One night I walked into a patient's room and noticed he was a county jail inmate in shackles.

I nodded at the Deputy and proceeded to get some vitals on this new arrival. The dude had a pirate patch over one of his eyes.

"Sir, what's going on? Why are you here tonight?" were the first words I spoke to him.

He seemed to not hear me, so I repeated the question.

The guy didn't stir. Just stared straight ahead with that one beady eye.

I noted a trail of clear fluid draining from under the patch and asked the Deputy, "Hey brother, what's this guy's story?"

He flashed a big grin and replied, "Dude, you ain't gonna believe this."

Adjusting in his chair he smiled and continued, "This guy had two eyes until a couple hours ago at which time he pulled one of them out and ate it."

I was speechless.

What does one say?

In the ER we learn to never brag, "Now, I've seen everything." Because there's always something crazy coming around the corner.

This was no exception, but this was also very high up there in the "disturbing" compartment.

I finished attaining the vitals and left the room.

Hours later, around 2am, I got a request from the RN to take this newly one-eyed guy up to CT for a quick scan of his head.

The dude freaked me out. I mean, he ate his own eye for crying out loud.

The hospital was old, mighty old, and the elevators slow and rickety. As it was the wee hours of the morning, we were the only ones in the elevator; the deputy, the prisoner and me.

As the doors creaked and shuddered closed, I pushed the proper button and moved back beside the patient.

God as my witness, and I know it was unprofessional, but I couldn't help but stare at that darn pirate patch. To make matters worse my curiosity was building.

I had so many questions. So naturally I asked, "Sir, I have to know, what did it taste like?"

With his gaze fixed on the door he replied with a gravelly voice straight out of Hollywood, "It tasted like fish. It was slimy and scaley."

I smiled. This was intense.

Before I could stop a second question leapt out of my mouth, "Sir, why did you eat your eyeball?"

With the voice of a wild man he boasted, "You know I'm a werewolf, right? I have wolf veins and I can run faster than any animal on the planet."

Ok, now this was too much! I was skeptical and challenged, "So, you're telling me you can run faster than a cheetah? A cheetah can run fifty-five miles an hour."

The guy took a few museful moments and replied, "Well, maybe not faster than a cheetah but faster than a coyote."

Wow! You just never knew what was coming through those Emergency Room doors.

Oh, and looks are indeed deceiving.

I once had a well-spoken and well-dressed patient who politely answered all questions asked of him. He was quite agreeable to anything the nursing staff requested. You know, one of those patients we thank God for, because he didn't monopolize our time.

Things began to pick up and the waiting room was soon filled. Pressure was on for the nurses to keep these patient orders completed and documentation up to date. One of the nurses I was helping asked, "Dennis do you mind hanging this bag of normal saline on that guy in bed 15?"

It was our friendly guy, and I was only too happy to hang fluids on a guy that would really appreciate it.

The nurse had already prepped the bag and IV line, so I only needed to step in, hang the fluids, hook them up to the IV port (after I had disinfected it) and then open it wide open.

That's how I envisioned the simple task.

Stepping into the room I greeted Mr. Friendly and lifted the bag up to hang it on the hook on the wall. It was not there.

I thought, "It was here earlier, because we had fluids hanging on the patient who occupied this space earlier in the shift."

What the heck?

I excused myself and looked around the department for a scarce IV pole.

Once back in the room I leaned forward, wiped the IV port and prepared to insert the line into the hub when I noticed a twinkling object in my periphery. This gentleman had a surgical incision in his abdomen. The stitches were there, and they looked to be healing nicely, but in the middle of the site was this twinkling object.

I looked closer and realized what it was, this dude had reached up to the wall, broken the hook off and stuck the whole hangar hook into his abdominal cavity through the days old surgical site.

Back to the OR he went for a good wash out and some exploration.

Having done this job for so long the stories all seem to jumble together and keeping them in chronological order becomes impossible. The realities of what human beings are capable of is staggering and made me question many things about my beliefs and the benevolence of life.

I recall a young lady who had come up short on a significant amount of drug money. Dangerous mistake.

She was kidnapped and for three months was tortured. There was not a square inch of her body that did not have a bruise, laceration, burn or wound in some state of healing.

Take her lacerations for example. Some of them were completely healed with only a thin white scar remaining as evidence. Others were scabbed over and were on track to completely heal in a week or so. Then there were other wounds that were fresh and still oozing blood.

Her neck had puncture marks from screw drivers and her buttocks, both left cheek and right, had full coil burns from a hot plate. Letters had been cut into the cheeks of her face.

The only reason she escaped was because one of her captors got careless with a cellphone and didn't realize that the young lady in question could wriggle out of her restraints.

The sight of her shook me.

The detectives who questioned her for hours held up 8x10 photos of some of the vilest looking people I'd ever seen in my life. Hard. These folks looked hard.

The detectives would ask, "Do you know who this is?"

Well, she knew who a lot of those people were, and she had a score to settle.

I tried leaving the room at one point to give her privacy, but she screamed, "No! Please don't leave me alone!"

Her nails dug into my arm. She was terrified.

"I won't leave you," I promised.

I remained with her for quite a while until she was transferred upstairs. I have no idea what happened to her, but I can't help but think that she was on borrowed time.

Slowly, day after day my world that had once been Cary Grant and Grace Kelly movies with happy endings, became shattered and I began to see the real world. It changed me. My innocence was gone forever and with it a large chunk of joy.

A darkness was building in my heart. Where once there was laughter, *I Love Lucy* episodes, and *Hogan's Heroes* now there was darkness, emptiness, and solitude. An invisible darkness was beginning to strengthen in my spirit. It found ways to feed itself and this involved leaching some of my greatest attributes: empathy, compassion, courage, and joyfulness.

As an empathetic caregiver I felt things very deeply. The attribute was vital in this field, but it was also a slippery slope into severe PTSD.

The Bear

When I was young and stupid, I thought of the homeless as the oddballs of society. Refuse. With the passing of time and the gift of life experience I came to learn that many of these women and men had steady jobs, college educations and successful careers...once upon a time.[59]

Life though had dealt them some heavy hands and these folks had folded. In my mature years I began to wonder, "How close am I to living on the streets?" One police ticket. One missed paycheck. One moment of poor decision and it could all be gone. It's a sobering thought.

Out of the hundreds of homeless that I came to know through the years one person stands out above the rest. He was a cantankerous old guy who reveled in giving the nurses a lot of grief. Much of the problem stemmed from the fact that he was always drunk.

Over time, I won him over and we had a lot of very interesting conversations.

---

[59] I then came to understand the pulverizing effects of mental illness that many of these folks suffer from. Untreated they wither on the vine, out of sight, dying, unnamed and unknown. It's a huge blight on our society that more is not done to help these folks.

His street name was Bear and he was originally from California. He was a graduate of UCLA and held a bachelor's degree in Engineering. World events interrupted his plans for the future though, and with the advent of Vietnam, he joined up and became an officer.

Word on the street was that he'd been decorated for valor and that his exploits were mentioned in Stars and Stripes magazine.[60] We couldn't fact check it at the time, but the story seemed to check out.

Bear returned from Vietnam having served honorably and got right to work. His education and letters of recommendation served him well and he soon had everything he desired; a wife, a daughter, and a six-figure income.

It was short lived.

Returning home from work he was surprised to find his wife's car was not in the garage. Working his way through the house he called out the names of his wife and daughter, but neither was home. In a panic he called relatives and friends, but no one had heard from her.

---

[60] A magazine printed for distribution among the service men and women of the US Armed Forces. The magazine had its birth during the Civil War and saw distribution in all the major wars since.

Hours later there was a knock at his door. It was the police, and they were there to report that both his wife and daughter had been killed by a drunk driver. His world crashed around him.

Everything he had worked for was for naught. He cared nothing for a home that would never again echo the laughter of his daughter or the teasing of his wife. He let it all go.

The job, house, car, bank account, everything meant nothing to him, He walked away and never looked back.

His only relief from this tragedy was found in the bottom of a bottle.

Living on the streets in southern California he soon tired of all the competition and began to walk and bum rides east. The passing of time only increased his surliness and soon those on the streets had given him his nickname, Bear.

He made his way to San Antonio where he settled down, working the churches, charities, shelters, and the street corners, "Flying a sign."[61]

---

[61] Street term for those who stand on street corners with cardboard signs asking for money or help. Of course it could be like the guy I saw in Austin whose sign displayed, "Why lie? I need a beer!" He made a killing.

Bear was no stranger to the Police and was regularly picked up for brawling and trespassing. Thing was though that he had a secret, "Get Out of Jail Free" card. Bear had a heart issue that always showed on the monitors of EMS.

So, any time that he got picked up by the Cops he'd start complaining, "Oh man fellas, my chest really hurts. You guys need to call me an ambulance."

The ambulance was called, monitor hooked up and sure enough, Bear's heart was in a horrendous looking rhythm. So, the Police would release him to the ambulance crew who would transport him to us.

We'd see him come through the Ambulance Bay doors on the stretcher a huge grin on his face. We'd just laugh.

One of the nurses would say, "Let me guess, you got picked up by the Police and started having chest pain."

He'd laugh, showing those toothless gums.

We'd just smile, nod our heads, and say, "All right Bear, you know the drill, time for an EKG and blood work."

He was as happy as could be. He had clean sheets and cute nurses to chat with and harass. About an hour into his stay with us would come the inevitable question, "Can I get a box lunch?"

During the times I'd draw his blood I took the opportunity to try and learn a little about him. This was how I found out about his service in Vietnam and tragedy of the loss of his family. I began calling him by the rank he attained in the Army, "Captain."

I'd see him come in, I'd salute, he'd return it crisply, expertly, and I'd ask, "Do you need anything Cap?"

He'd shake his head and reply "Nah, I'm ok."

This went on for months and soon others in the ER began to refer to him by his rank. He appreciated it. His eyes would glisten as memories of days long gone came flooding back.

Then suddenly Bear just never came around. We were concerned that something may have happened to him on the streets. Perhaps his old ticker had finally given out on him.

Months later we were surprised to see him come in on a stretcher wearing an orange-colored Bexar County Jail jump suit.

One of the nurses asked, "What the heck happened Bear?"

The chastened character mumbled, "Ah, the police picked me up for trespassing again. This time the judge got tired of seeing me and put me away for a couple months."

Truth be told, this was the best we'd seen Bear look in a very long time. He was required to shower, made to take his medications daily, was getting solid meals and great sleep. He looked amazing! His cheeks were rose red, even plump and his countenance was remarkable. He was incredibly lucid and quite the conversationalist.

Taking his blood pressure I said, "Hey Captain, there's a new Mel Gibson movie that just came out called *We Were Soldiers*. It's about Vietnam. I'm going to give you my number and when you get out of jail give me a call. We'll grab something to eat and go see it. What do you say?"

Bear smiled, nodded his head and replied, "That sounds real fine. I'd like that."

I wrote my number on his discharge papers and told him to call me when he was released from jail.

Months went by and no phone call.

Then came the word.

While conducting bed checks at the County Jail, one of the deputies discovered Bear, lying comfortably in his bed, all tucked in. He had died in his sleep. The old warrior's heart had finally given up the struggle.

It hit us hard, but we took solace in the fact that when he came to our Emergency Department he was treated as a man. He was a UCLA graduate. An Engineer. He was a husband. A father. A Captain in the Army and a decorated war hero. He was treated with respect and dare I say, we loved him.

Here's to you Captain.[62]

---

[62] Everything within me wanted to put down his real name. I know there is probably not a person on the planet that would object. However, there are HIPPA laws, and I must respect them.

Memorial Day Weekend

I knew this shift was going to be busy for four reasons.

First, it was Friday, and the end of the work week was always busy.

Second, it was the first day of Memorial Day weekend.

Third, it was a city-wide high school graduation night.

To top it all off it was a full moon.

It was the perfect storm. A recipe for disaster.

I'd been off the day before, so I'd not seen the schedule assignments. After parking my car and walking up "Cardiac Hill" to get to the ER I had no idea just how busy it was about to get.

I passed through the Ambulance Bay doors and immediately heard the EMS radio in triage blaring the report of some inbound unit. One of the day shift medics saw me and made a straight path to me.

He looked serious, "Dennis, clock in and go to the helipad, you have one coming in and she sounds bad off."

I replied, "I take it this means I'm in Trauma tonight."

He nodded his head and quipped, "Yep."

My heart began to race. I clocked in, bypassed our Shift Huddle, and made my way straight up to the helipad.

I could see the small dot on the horizon heading in, passing over Six Flags. As it drew closer my hands began to sweat. I was nervous. No matter, I had a bird inbound. It was "go" time.

Soon the helicopter was less than a minute out. I pulled my goggles down over my eyes, plugged my ears with the hearing protection, and slid on two pairs of medical gloves.

I leaned over once again to look under the stretcher, just to be sure the oxygen tank was full.

It was.

Wump! Wump! Wump!

Violent downdrafts flashed across the concrete helipad causing bits of paper and dust to fly in all directions.[63] I leaned into the wind.

Soon a flight nurse emerged from the side of the chopper, secured the door open, looked my way, and gave me the "thumbs up" sign.

As I approached, I noticed a stream of blood was leaking out the door and a small scarlet pool had begun to form on the concrete.

In a matter of seconds, we had her on my stretcher and were making our way to the elevator that would take us to the ground floor. The flight nurse, who was bagging the patient, looked at the monitor and said, "Check her pulse. I think we just lost it."

The flight medic reached up and sure enough, no pulse. He leapt up on the stretcher, straddled her, and began to do chest compressions.

The elevator doors opened, and we began our trek across a small access road which security had blocked off

---

[63] We never had a stretcher mattress or sheets with us for they could be lifted up into the blades causing a calamitous situation.

for us. Then it was up the last bit of "Cardiac Hill" huffing and puffing.

I was sweating like crazy, but adrenaline boosted my strength. My mind raced trying to prioritize all the procedures and equipment that this young lady would require. I was snapped out of my thoughts when one of our hospital policemen jogged up, grabbed hold of the stretcher, and helped me push it up the hill.

A cool blast of air greeted us as we crossed the threshold through the Ambulance Bay. I heard one of the nurses in triage call out, "Hey, call Trauma, they're doing CPR on this one."

There was a bit of a rush at first because in the code room they were expecting a 22-year-old female with a pulse. Suddenly we burst on the scene doing CPR. This changed everything.

Orders to the clerk were called out over the report given by the air crew:

"Call Blood Bank, tell them we need crash blood STAT!"

"Call Pharmacy, tell them we're going to need more meds down here!"

Meanwhile I heard one of the doctors call out, "Get me a thoracotomy tray!"

Yikes!

A Trauma Resident was handed a 21-blade scalpel and then an incision was made between the ribs. This was a long incision, at least ten inches in length. Blood squirted out of the opened skin splattering against the doctor's blue impervious gown. Sterile metallic rib spreaders were brought out, shoved between two ribs and a crank was manipulated causing the ribs to separate, revealing the left lung and heart.

As I was on the left side of the patient, standing beside her, hooking up the metallic "spoons" to the defibrator[64], I could see her organs quite clearly. The heart sat motionless.

Blood covered the floor. Alarms from the monitor, IV pump, and rapid infuser were all sounding off. A bloody gloved hand reached up, grabbed the overhead light, flipped it on, and moved it so it shown directly into the open chest cavity.

---

[64] When shocking the heart externally against the skin we use the paddles one sees in movies, or more commonly we use plastic pads with goop that stick to the patient's chest and flank. When shocking a patient internally we use metal spoon shaped utensils that are placed directly against the heart. A much smaller dose of electricity is used in this case. Unless you want barbacoa.

The Attending Surgeon used a sterile hemostat to clamp a squirting vessel in the chest while the Trauma Resident moved her gloved hand across the heart, aorta, arteries, and other vessels looking for injuries, lacerations, or small bleeders.

Meds were pushed, crash blood was infused through the rapid infuser, one unit, a second unit and then a third. Meanwhile the Trauma Resident was manually compressing the heart with her gloved hands inside the chest.

Suddenly the resident called out, "Hey we got activity here!"

We all could plainly see the heart was beating. The Attending then called out, "Call OR, tell them we're on the way!"

One of the medics sprinted down the hall and called up the Trauma Elevator and held it for us. We liked this elevator because it had oxygen hook ups, suction, and various supplies. The other medic offered to accompany the team to OR so I could start getting the room squared away.

The floor of the trauma bay was absolutely littered with debris: wrappers, gloves, bits of clothing, large blood clots, pools of blood, empty liter bags of blood, and torn clothing.

I quickly switched out the suction tanks, replaced the Yankauers[65] and tubing, wiped down the knobs. I then grabbed the push broom and swept all the debris into a big bloody pile. With gloved hands I scooped up the pile and discarded it into a garbage can that was lined with a red biohazard bag.

Housekeeping hurried in and began to mop up the blood and sanitize the floor. Meanwhile I removed the sharps[66] from the Chest Tube Trays, Thoracotomy Tray and made sure the Central Line trays didn't hide any solo needles or scalpels. Trauma Residents were notorious for leaving sharps around. The nurses fussed at them all the time about that.

The phone rang and I watched as an RN quickly jotted down notes. She said nothing until the end, "How far out?"

She hung up, looked at me and said, "Dennis, you have another patient coming in by air, five minutes out another traumatic arrest, CPR is in progress."

---

[65] A suction tip device that goes into a patients mouth to remove secretions, vomit, blood or foreign objects.
[66] These included needles and scalpels

I called out, "Got it!"

I grabbed a stretcher in the hall, tore off the mattress and tossed it to the side. I checked the O2 tank and then set off for the parking garage whose top hosted our helipad.

"Make a hole! Make a hole!" I shouted as I made my way down the crowded hallway and then out into the dark of night. In the distance I could hear the faint, deep bass throb of the helicopter on approach.

I raced down the hill, punched in the code for the elevator, made it to the top just in time to see the metallic bird about fifty feet off the platform.

Once we had the patient on my stretcher, we made way for the elevator. The crew had been doing CPR on this young lady for quite a while, so I volunteered to take over. The flight nurse nodded approval, and I stepped up on the stretcher, straddled the patient and began to do chest compressions.

Each time I thrust down her head would sway back and forth, left and then right, with the force. Her eyelids were halfway open and there was a cloudy film developing over them.

Every once in a while the flight nurse would compress the Ambu-Bag forcing oxygen into this young ladies' lungs. It was the same scene as only an hour before. Both young ladies were in their mid-twenties.

When we entered the Trauma Bay one of the flight crew began calling out the report. As I stepped down one of the other ER techs took over CPR for me. She utilized a stool beside the stretcher because the surgeons would need access to our patient's chest.

I immediately began setting up two Pleur-evacs[67] for the Chest Tubes that were called for.

I was bending down beside the patient's head, positioning the equipment when I heard a squish sound. I turned to look at the young lady who was mere inches from my face. Each time the medic pushed down with a chest compression blood would shoot out of the patient's nose and left ear. Soon the fluid coming out of the ear was clear. It was obvious she had massive skull fractures for the cerebrospinal fluid was leaking out.

This was a losing battle and after a few more minutes it was decided to call it quits. She could not be saved.

---

[67] Rectangular plastic containers that hook to the side of the bed. These are connected to suction from the wall which pulls blood and air from the pleural cavity thus allowing the lungs to fill to their full capacity.

We turned off the ventilator and the monitor and began unhooking the equipment. The smell of iron was thick in the air. The only sounds were the active suction canisters, the monitor alarm, and the rapid infuser. Standing at the cardiac monitor I printed two rhythm strips, the code summary and then turned it off.

Meanwhile a few other techs had come in to help me clean and restock the room. The teamwork was awesome as always.

There was so much blood under and around her body that we decided it would be easier to clean her up if we moved her to a different stretcher. This was done and we were able to make her presentable should family stop by to see her. The original stretcher was wiped down with towels and then I wheeled it outside to the Ambulance Bay and hosed it off.

Watching the red streams of water coursing down the asphalt to the grass my mind began to wander. I couldn't help but wonder how many thousands of people's DNA could be found in the soil there. It was an odd passing thought.

It had only been two hours and we had ten to go!

Soon the floor was mopped, the monitors sanitized, the IV carts were stocked and…

The phone rang, triage calling.

The RN took out a pen and began to take down notes.

As she finished, she exclaimed to the busy room, "We've got two coming in by air. Head-on collision. Two deaths on scene. Five-year-old not doing well. Female passenger of the other vehicle has an obvious femur fracture but is stable. Thirty minutes out!"

So, before we delve into this next case, let me first tell you what happened to the patients we were receiving. I'll describe the cars involved in the accident as Car "A" and Car "B".

Car "A" is a family of six, a husband and wife and four children. They are heading home after partying with family. The husband is quite drunk, so the wife begs him to let her drive, but he angrily yells, "Get in the car or so help me I'll smack you around!"

The guy puts the car in reverse and begins to back up, but all the kids are not in yet. The wife screams, "Wait, we're not in yet!"

The guy came inches from running over his three-year-old son. The wife knows better than to ask again if she can drive. She sits in the front and prays they make it safely home.

Car "B" is also a family who had been out visiting relatives at a Memorial Day BBQ. In the front compartment of this vehicle is the father who is driving and the wife next to him. In the rear compartment is a nine-month-old baby secure in a car seat. Next to her sits her five-year-old brother who is also secure in his seat.

As the sober father drives, the family talks about what a great time they had. It had been a long day of fun and before too long everyone is asleep, except for the dad of course.

On a lone rural Texas road, the two cars approach each other from different directions. The drunk driver in Car "A" swerves right into the path of the family in Car "B." The accumulative force is staggering.

In Car "B" the mother is instantly killed as is the nine-month-old baby. The five-year-old is barely clinging to life. He is packaged into a helicopter and on his way to us. The father in Car "B" is slightly injured and taken to a local rural hospital by ambulance.

All the children in Car "A" survive with minor injuries and are taken to local hospitals where they are treated and released. The wife in Car "A" has a fractured femur and is airlifted to us. The drunk driver was airlifted to another Trauma Center and as such I was unaware of his condition.

We worked on the kindergarten-aged boy for quite a while. We managed to get him somewhat stabilized and sent him to the OR. From there he was transferred to the Pediatric ICU but five days later he died.

I made a mistake. I thought about the implications of this night on the father who had done nothing wrong. He'd taken his family for a day of fun with relatives. No doubt the nine-month-old baby was doted on. I imagined other relatives saying to the older child, "My, look how much you've grown!"

My mind wandered as I sat outside under the stars. I needed to get out of there, listen to the sounds of the night, watch the lights of the city twinkle in all directions. Life went on and yet for some it did not.

Unfortunately, I imagined this poor utterly destitute father opening the door to his home that was now deathly silent. Toys on the carpet, baby bottles drying on the dish rack, his wife's "To Do List" on the fridge all served as a cruel reminder of a life he no longer had.

How does a dad survive that? There's no way I could live there. Everything would be a reminder of loss. The fact that my homeless guy Bear had walked away from everything made more sense to me. I could see how that would be the only option.

A darkness that had been gradually taking root inside of me now grew stronger. Remember the journal I kept. Well, this would mark the last time I'd make an entry regarding what I'd seen. Fittingly, the day already had an official title, Memorial Day.

A few months later, on Veteran's Day, November 11, 1999, I officially closed out my journal with a final entry.

Here's what I wrote,

It is amazing the change that has occurred during the progress of this short diary of my ER experiences. At first you notice I don't miss a day. I talk of doing EKG's and irrigating lacerations and even drawing blood.

After awhile the space between entries widens. I no longer chart what I see, though I've seen and still do see bad stuff. For instance it is now November and the last time I bothered to chart was May. Wow, I have changed. This will probably be my last ER entry unless something very extraordinary happens.

Indeed, it was my last entry.

The Dark Passenger

At the time of this writing, it's been almost two years since I retired from the ER.

No, "retired" is not the right word for that makes it sound like I had a send-off party, complete with a plaque thanking me for my twenty-three years in Emergency Medicine. That's definitely not how it went down.

There was no room full of people clapping me on the back and wishing me luck on my next ventures. No clinking of wine glasses. Absent was the raucous laughter as hilarious stories were retold.

In fact, the last day of my ER epoch came to end with an Uber ride, the sound of broken glass, and trips to multiple doctors. Ironic.

But that was at the end of my career.

Rewinding about fourteen years would take me to a time and place where I truly became aware of a startling fact, I had a serious problem brewing in my brain.

The symptoms were clear enough; change in personality, inability to sleep through the night, unfulfillment with life pursuits and seemingly no hope for the future. The future? Why bother with something so far away.

I still felt joy inside, but it was deep, way deep down and seriously felt like it was buried, no, that's not right…it was submerged under a thick black oily layer of fear and dread that was seldom penetrated.

I used to describe this somberness in a way that Dexter, a character on a Showtime television show of the same name described it. It was his **"Dark Passenger."** I loved that description for it was exactly how I felt.

My mother and sisters asked me, "Where'd your smile go?"

I'd make up some excuse about not feeling well for I didn't have the heart to tell them that the Dennis they used to know was disappearing. That truth terrified me because I didn't want to disappear. I wanted to be present in life. I just didn't know how to stop myself from plunging deeper into the darkness. The light was leaving my eyes.

On rare occasions I'd try to explain the darkness, but good Christian families start to get nervous and stir in their seats. So I tamed it down, brushed it off and framed a smile on my face.

I believed they weren't ready for the full unedited version. Truthfully though, I spared my mother the true extent of my darkness for she is such a kind, loving person and I didn't want to trouble or upset her.[68]

Dad had seen war, saw men die and was involved with the killing of the enemies of our country. He knew all about the darkness and we had some very candid conversations about it. He was and always has been my hero and to hear that he was dealing with the same stuff meant a lot to me.

Still though, that didn't help with my problem. I needed a major rewiring of my brain and dad couldn't help with that.

On one occasion I was particularly bitter and let loose on my folks. They wanted to know what was wrong, so I'd tell them. I wasn't angry. I guess I was just exhausted and wanted them to finally see just what I'd been dealing with.

So, how did I explain "The Darkness" to my family?

Well, that conversation went something like this, "Mom and Dad from birth you provided me with a

---

[68] Looking back, I absolutely should have poured my heart out to them. They were the few people on this planet who loved me unconditionally.

beautiful life. I've never wanted for anything. There's always been warmth and tons of love."

"Your protection, the life lessons, the morality, my conscience and character were all tended and molded over many years by you both. The product of all of this labor and love was a strong guard, a protective case that completely surrounded my heart."

"When I prepared the body of a two-year-old girl for her family to come view her, a tiny pinpoint chisel was raised to the guard around my heart. Then a tiny hammer struck this invisible chisel a single time. In that instant a small, imperceptible fleck of that guard chipped away and flew off into oblivion."

"I once stood in the void between two sisters who were eight and three years old. I helped do CPR on both of them."

"Sprinting up flights of stairs to retrieve 'crash blood' for those little girls my chest heaved for oxygen. As I topped the stairs and sprinted down the long hallway to the Blood Bank I shouted, 'Make a hole! Coming through!' I'd then sprint back down the flights of stairs taking them four or five steps at a time."

"With sweat pouring down my neck and back I handed the blood off to a nurse and jumped in again to take over CPR for the other medic. When the desperate Trauma Faculty Surgeon couldn't get a central line on the younger sister I blurted out, 'How about a cutdown tray?' The tray was opened, a deep incision in the groin made, the blood vessel revealed, and a central line attained. It was of no use though and we all knew it. We'd known it for a long time, but no one wanted to quit."

"We fought against the impossible and the room fell silent as the Trauma Resident looked to the Attending for guidance. We all knew what needed to be done. The Attending made that fateful turn of the head toward the clock, oh that diligent clock that kept on ticking, and said, 'Time of death…'"

"The three-year-old was worked a little longer and then she too was pronounced dead."

I fell silent, remembering the scene, and then continued, "I stepped through large pools of toddler blood that stuck to my shoes and made suction sounds as I walked. The intense iron smell of their precious blood assaulted my nose. All the while I could hear the drunk driver who'd slammed into their car cursing the medical staff, demanding pain meds."

"I saw the trails of bloody foot-prints running from the code room to the lab, to X-ray, and to the nursing station. Standing there, taking in the scene, trying to catch my breath, right then, amidst that horrific scene that same rusty chisel was placed against the guard of my heart. Then came the swing of the unfeeling cold hammer held by the Dark Passenger. A tiny fleck of the guard that had been so loving placed around my heart spun off into the darkness."

Tears fell as I tried to explain what was happening to me.

I went on, "How do I take a wound dressing, roll it up, stick it into a small child's cracked skull and remain untouched? I mean, logically, if I don't plug the hole her parents are going to freak out because the brains are coming out like playdoh. Her ICP (intercranial pressure) is so great that her swelling brain has nowhere else to go. So, I do the humane thing, I stick my finger into her skull, stop the morbid spillage, rinse the gray matter and blood clots out of her hair, wrap her head with gauze, change the sheets and prep the room for the family to come view their daughter."

"My only companions this whole time; the musty swamp water aroma of brains, the chisel, the hammer and the **Dark Passenger**."

I have children of my own so I can imagine how horrific it was for my parents to truly grasp what was actively happening to me deep inside. I was so thankful for their love and support, but the malevolent darkness remained.

Sometimes the **Dark Passenger** would raise a grizzly hand and yank my brain causing me to fall into a funk. This usually happened when I'd catch a smell of iron or of diesel. Perhaps a child in a grocery store reminded me of one of the many children I had to prep for viewing. On such occasions my anger would flare. I'd lash out at family or friends in unwarranted wrath that didn't match the setting. I distanced myself from good friends; Will, Becky, Jennifer, Roger, Rebecca, Tom, Candelario, Shawn, Joanne, Mark, Lety and others. I was slowly, relentlessly drowning.

Days turned to weeks, and you know the rest of that progression. The next thing I knew it had been years and I'd seen hundreds of adults and children die from stabbings, horse riding accidents, drowning, heart attacks, strokes, child neglect, murder, electric shock, human trafficking, burns, torture, hanging, shootings, toxic ingestion, old age and a myriad of other deaths.

All the while that tiny hammer kept on swinging. Day after day. The inaudible clang of the strikes on the chisel were noticed by no one, not even me. My zest for life diminished. No longer was I going out with friends. I'd rather stay home in a dark quiet room and watch a movie.

Now, reader, let's take a break but don't dare put this book down. This is not the ramblings of a dispirited dude with a history of depression. I'm not trying to smother you with sorrow or to bequeath my inner pain to you. My intent is to make you aware of what happened to me, and to then conversely insight in you an understanding that perhaps this is happening to the RN's, Medic's, Firemen and Police in your neighborhood.

I know this chapter is hard to read, but that's the point isn't it. No one held a gun to my head and forced me to sign up for the job. I knew that death was going to be a companion, but I just never could have imagined the full extent of the numbers I'd see.

The experience began to imprint on all my senses and would soon burn itself into my spirit. With each hammer blow on my heart, I grew less and less hopeful for the future. Then, without realizing it, I stopped planning on the future.

I eventually had to leave the Level One Trauma Center. It was just too much. I couldn't bear it anymore. Thus came an end to twelve years in the Trauma Center. I didn't know it then, but I had ten more ER years to go.

Part Three

Dire Straits

A New ER

One thing was certain, I needed out of the trauma center. The troubling factor was that I only knew Emergency Medicine. I had never done anything else. I hoped that if I transferred to an ER on the outskirts of the city the exposure to such horrific scenes would be minimal. The sort of ER where a stabbing is the result of a failed attempt to dice an onion and not from a murder attempt. A place where a gunshot victim comes in once a year and is thus big news.

I was naïve. More to the point, perhaps I was willfully blind. The very nature of Emergency Medicine guaranteed that I'd be exposed to death, pain, and suffering. However, I trudged ahead with my grand scheme and set off for one such hospital, hoping to get an interview.

So, I put on my suit and tie and drove across town to the affluent part of San Antonio. I dropped in on a small hospital's tiny Human Resources department. I'd not filled out an application and had not called ahead so they were unaware I even existed. I was just going to show up and see what would happen.

I approached the desk and in a matter of seconds the one and only HR employee came out. I asked if there were any openings. The kind young lady responded that she didn't know but she would call the ER Director and ask.

While on the phone the clerk, paused, looked over at me and asked, "Do you have any experience?"

I said, "Yes ma'am, twelve years in a Level One Trauma Center."

My reply was relayed and then the phone was hung up.

"Mr. Blocker," she said, "The ER Director asked if you don't mind waiting a few minutes she'll be down here."

A few minutes later the door opened, and I was introduced to the Director. She was awesome, tremendous energy. I walked with her to the ER and after taking a seat in her office, she asked their senior Medic/Tech to join us.

Introductions were made and she said, "So, Dennis, tell us about yourself."

I replied, "Well, I worked twelve years in a Level One Trauma Center. Being on the Trauma Team I know how to prime and then zero arterial lines. The Level One Rapid Infuser was something that we used quite often so I am also proficient in its operation and troubleshooting. I'm proficient with IV sticks and cool during Codes.

I explained my duties and told a few stories to make them laugh. Look, let's be real, I was trying to make myself too valuable to pass up. However, a few minutes into my speech a horrible thought crossed my mind, "Perhaps they think I'm overqualified."

I needn't have worried for as I spoke their mouths hung open. The director looked over at the medic, smiled, and then asked, "Do you think you could train us to do all that stuff if we hire you?"

We all laughed but then she quickly added, "Seriously though, can you train us?"

I answered, "Yes ma'am, I'd be glad to."

She then asked, "Are you free to work any shifts."

This was a point I was not willing to bend on. By this point in my life I had two daughters at home. There was no way I'd not be home at night to put them to bed and be there if they had a nightmare.

I replied, "No ma'am. Days are the only option. I have kids and need to be home with them at night."

The ER Director looked over at the senior Tech/Medic and then back at me. She extended her hand and said, "Welcome aboard."

And just like that I was hired.

Funny thing. I had to go back to Human Resources and fill out an application. This was probably one of the most unusual hires I've ever had. I was thankful for the employment, encouraged they had seen my worth, and looking forward to a new facility with less death and better pay. I could finally begin the process of healing my battered brain.

Well, at least that was the plan.

As it was a smaller hospital, the facility relied heavily on the experience of those who worked the ER. This meant that any shift I worked I was required to respond with an ER doctor and RN to emergencies throughout the entire hospital, including the ICU.

You can imagine what this did to the darkness that flowed under my skin. I'd be walking down the hall and hear the page tones over the hospital speakers followed by, "Code Blue, Third Floor, Room Three Zero Two. Code Blue, Third Floor, Room Three Zero Two."

I'd run to the ER, grab an airway box, a bougie[69] and an Ambu bag. Meanwhile a nurse would pull the intubation medication box from the Pyxis[70] and we'd meet up with the ER Doc at the Elevators. I usually grabbed the LUCAS as well.[71]

In this small hospital the floor nurses were always glad to see us. I had of course worked hard to build bridges with them, so I knew them all. They'd see us walk in the door and I'd hear, "Oh thank God you guys are here."

It felt awesome that the floor staff nurses trusted us and felt calm when we arrived. Ever the teacher, I'd try and get them involved so they could learn from these experiences. Ever in the back of my mind was the abysmal orientation I'd been given in the Trauma Center all those years before.

These opportunities to save lives always brought the best out of me and it was the few times I felt like I was

---

[69] A two-foot-long stiff plastic wand that is placed down a patient's trachea to secure an airway. Basically, it is a place saver, a "guidewire" for an endotracheal tube which is inserted between the vocal cords and then advanced about two centimeters.
[70] A fridge like appliance that is locked and can only be opened when a Registered Nurse signs into the Pyxis via a fingerprint scan and password. The nurse is then able to pull the medications from a drawer that the computer opens for the RN. This prevents medication errors.
[71] An easy-to-use mechanical chest compression device that helps lifesaving teams deliver high-quality chest compressions during CPR. These devices worked great! I even had two patients come back from the dead and sit up with this machine thumping on their chest.

making a difference. Once again though, the inherent problem was that being around this pain, suffering and death was stoking my inner darkness.

In the months and years that followed I'd make many friends and take part in some interesting cases. As I worked and sought to maintain my mental discipline the darkness was always there on the periphery. Waiting. Watching. It was exhausting but I had little ones depending on me so I "embraced the suck.[72]"

---

[72] The awesome phrase is generally credited to Colonel Austin Bay of the US Army and means, "The situation is bad, but deal with it."

Tough Guy Tears

I stepped into a patient room to get vital signs on a new arrival. The IV had been started by EMS and the nurse had already drawn the blood so there was nothing else that needed to be done.

Entering the room, I noted a woman who looked to be in her early forties lying on the bed sleeping. Her mouth was open, and saliva was oozing from the corner of her mouth.

I watched her chest rise and fall and was happy she was resting peacefully.

A gentleman sitting in the room noticed my discerning eye and said, "She had a seizure on the way in. That's why she's sleeping so hard."

As he spoke, I noticed his face seemed careworn. His countenance was steeped in concern and tempered with resolution. The eyes told a story of sleepless nights and dread of the future.

I recognized something else in those windows to his soul. Something old, bitter, dark…familiar. These were the eyes of a man who'd seen death, misery, and all sorts of human suffering.

I asked, "What line of work are you in sir? If I was to guess I'd say you're a policeman."

He chuckled, "Wow. Yeah. I'm a detective with homicide. How could you tell?"

I turned from what I was doing, looked him straight on and said, "I saw it in your eyes."

Water immediately came to those eyes. Not a lot and certainly not enough to cause a tear to fall, but well-up they did.

A few seconds of silence and I added, "We've seen a lot haven't we."

He sighed heavily and nodded his head as he admitted, "Yeah, we have. Too much I think."

The hardened detective went on to tell how his wife of so many years was dying and that there was nothing that could be done. A brain tumor was taking the love of his life and he was powerless.

My heart felt for the man. It was obvious he loved her. His strength, fortitude, street smarts and ability with his fists were of no use against this hidden enemy that was slowly robbing his wife of her essence.

I closed the door so we could talk privately. I had a feeling that he wanted to say something but was too embarrassed to talk freely in front of the ladies.

As the door closed, he looked at me and said in a mocking way, "I guess there's a reason for everything."

He was bitter and I knew it was not a sincere statement. Anger and loss were stealing his wife, pilfering his joy. It would have been more fitting for him to throw the chair across the room and shout at the ceiling with a clenched fist, "THIS IS NOT RIGHT! WHY HER?"

Instead, he had shoved those emotions and thoughts down into a secret part of his heart and let them stew and fester. My guess is that they had children together and he was adept at being strong for them.

I looked over at him and said something I'd never told another human, "Sir, sometimes life just friggin sucks. There's no reason or purpose for this."

The detective burst into tears and let the flood gates open. He sobbed and sobbed.

I put a box of tissues near him and gave his shoulder a man pat.

With tears streaming down his face, this tough and hardened homicide detective said, "You have no idea how bad I needed to hear those words. I'm so tired of people telling me, 'There's a reason for everything.' Why? What is the reason for this? Why take such a wonderful mother from her kids, from me? You're so right. Thank you so much."

I put my hand on his shoulder, patted it, and stepped outside closing the door behind me.

I was glad I could provide comfort to someone who had no illusions about what the near future held. I knew that detectives too have their own Dark Passengers.

Empathy. Compassion. Meanwhile, my own passenger had another opportunity to hit that chisel, driving that spike closer to my heart. It was only a matter of time now and that guard around my heart would fail.

The Streak

Even in these dark days there were moments of levity. One day I heard a nurse call over our handheld radios that she had a suicidal teenage boy who was being difficult. The kid was refusing to get into a hospital gown.

As I stepped up to the room, I heard him cursing at his mother.

I threw open the curtain, adopted my Conan the Barbarian voice and shouted, "Knock off cussing your mother dude. You should be ashamed of yourself. Get into this friggin gown right now or I'm gonna cut every stitch of clothing off you myself and dress you like a child."

He tried to sound like a man, "You can't do that!"

I took out my shears, snapped them a couple times and said, "Oh, try me and find out how fast those clothes come flying off your body bub."

The teen begrudgingly took off his clothes, striped down to his underwear and slipped on the gown.

As I stepped out of the room he mouthed off to his mom and the nurse rebuked him, "Hey! That's uncalled for. Don't you talk to your mother like that."

I heard this stellar human drop an "F" bomb and then I heard the nurse yell, "Where do you think you're going!"

Next thing I know I hear the nurse exclaim, "Get him! He's running! Don't let him go! He's a minor!"

Ah crud! Warp speed engage! I bolted after this seventeen-year-old jack rabbit.

Down the hall we sprinted. When we came to a "T" junction he had to slow and as he turned right, I reached out for his waist. My fingers slid along his pelvic bone and caught on the band of his underwear.

You see, when he bolted out of the room, he threw off his gown. He was sprinting through the ER wearing only his Fruit of the Looms.

Now when my fingers slipped and fell to his waist band, I grabbed what I could and "rrrrrriiiiippppp" there goes the underwear.

Ah crap! Now I've got a teenager free balling through the ER doing his best Carl Lewis.[73] Unbelievably, the teen

---

[73] A tremendous US Olympian who won nine gold medals in Track and Field.

254

was sprinting for the outside world which he now spied through the Ambulance Bay doors just a few feet ahead.

He hits those doors hard, and they flew wide open, but I was right on his heels.

With a swift lunge I pushed my hands forward against his elbows which caused them to fly up and forward across his chest. I grabbed his forearms from behind, lifted him up off the ground and walked him back to the ER.

Now, picture this, here I'm walking this free balling seventeen-year-old pasty white kid back into the ER. God and country can see everything, but there's nothing that can be done for now. He'd made his choice.

With his feet a few inches off the ground he's going where I want to go, and that's to his mother's side. As we pass by one of the treatment rooms I hear an elderly lady call out in a cracking, weathered voice, "Never a dull moment in this place!"

Somewhere in Time

I stepped into a room to start an IV on a lady who was going to need some IV fluids administered. The fact that she also needed some blood drawn meant that I could take care of two tasks at the same time.

Per my usual custom I announced myself at the door and stepped in, greeting her warmly.

The elderly lady had one of those smiles that just makes you think of homemade cookies and warm fires with cocoa in your mug. I instantly liked her.

Stepping over to the right side of the stretcher I asked her name and birthday. While she gave me the answers, I held her wrist band in hand and said, "Oh, I see from your birthday that you were in your twenties during the War. Do you recall what you were doing when you heard about Pearl Harbor?"

She smiled, nodded her head, and told me but her answer is lost to my memory banks. However, it was what followed that struck me to my core.

She said, "My husband was a pilot. In the Pacific. His plane went down in June of 1944, and they never found his plane."

Anyone who knows me understands that World War II is my favorite subject, so I was instantly her pupil.

I asked, "What sort of plane did he fly? Was he shot down?"

This kind lady looked down at her hands and gently rubbed them together. Memories flooding her mind. I wondered if I'd overstepped.

Her soft voice replied, "He flew a P-38. Have you heard of those?"

I was beaming, "Yes ma'am I sure have. Those are the kind of fighter plane with the double tail fins."

She laughed, "Well, you know your stuff. For someone so young how is it that you are interested in the subject?"

I told her of one of my heroes, my grandpa Lemke, who had served in the Pacific. I related to her my efforts to preserve WWII history these past many years and just so she would know I knew my stuff I started dropping some Big Band group names: Artie Shaw, Benny Goodman,

Louis Armstrong, Glenn Miller, Jimmy Dorsey, Louis Prima, and of course Harry James.

Her eyes lit up and she giggled. She never dreamed she'd be talking to a young person about music groups from the days of her youth.

This lovely lady looked over at me and said, "My husband's plane developed some trouble. He radioed to his wingman that he was going to try and find a spot to land. His buddies saw him descend into a cloudbank and he was not heard from again."

"I'm so sorry to hear that ma'am," was my weak, inadequate reply.

She then said, "But that was not the end of his story. I was recently contacted by the government that an Australian man had been scouring the jungles of Guadalcanal, looking for my husband's plane. The searcher had several reports that indicated the basic location where my husband was seen to go down."

I was intrigued.

She continued, "This Australian, using his own finances, used pumps to drain a portion of swamp he suspected contained the aircraft. Sure enough, he noticed a shiny metallic glint from the swamp. He rushed over and cleared away the weeds and muck and there was one of the tailfins of my husband's aircraft."

She paused, looked down at the IV in her arm and continued, "This man worked his way to where the cockpit was, cleaned off as much as he could, looked inside and saw that my husband was still in there. He didn't open it but contacted the authorities who then took over the recovery."

Her voice cracked and she looked out the door to some place far off and said, "You know, for me he's always twenty-eight years old. I look in the mirror and see an old lady. But he never ages."

Tears coursed down my cheeks.

I asked, "So, is he home now?"

She sighed and said, "Yes, in fact his funeral is going to be in December."

I perked up, "Oh! So, are you going?"

With a tired voice, that hinted at years of sorrow she'd hidden in a secret place in her heart, she replied, "No, my health is not too good, but my sons are going to go and represent me."

She looked over at me and said, "My boys are from my marriage after the War."

I shook her hand and thanked her for telling me that story from her life.

You just never know who you are taking care of. In the ER we are always rushing here and there, meeting timetables and checking off tasks. Yet, sitting there, inches away is someone with an amazing story to tell.

Perhaps it's the hopeless romantic in me, but anytime I think of this story I always hear the theme music of *"Somewhere in Time"* play in my mind.

Gosh, what an amazing story and how many more are out there, somewhere in time.

Major Peyton S. Mathis
United States Army Air Corps
Died June 5th 1944

Australian Anders Markwarth rests a hand on the tail fin of Major Mathis aircraft.

A Case for Experience

I was stocking IV carts and making rounds on the nurses making sure they were doing ok.

Our clerk called out over the radio, "Hey Dennis, a nurse from the MACU (Minor Acute Care Unit)[74] is wondering if you can go back there and take care of an EKG issue they're having."

I pressed the transmit button on my radio, "Roger that. Heading over there now."

Such requests usually have to do with changing the paper on the EKG machine which is not that intuitive. So, I made my way over and all the while contemplated what kind of taco I was going to order from the cafeteria when I was done.

A nurse hears the doors mechanical arms operate and peeks out of her room. She smiles and waves me over.

Just as I suspected she says, "Hey Dennis I'm having a heck of a time changing out this paper."

---

[74] This is a unit of about eight rooms that borders the ER and is a place we would move admitted patients who were waiting for a room upstairs.

I smile and reply, "No worries. I'll get you squared away."

With the paper loaded I ask the nurse, "Would you like me to run the EKG. You know, since I'm here and ready to go."

The nurse immediately replies, "Yes, be ready to run it continuous."

I think, "Wait? What?"

Now, let's back up a minute or so. When I entered the room, I smiled at the patient and wished her a, "Good morning."

I'd not looked around to see who else was in the room. I could see human forms standing around, but it wasn't my business. I was there to make as little footprint as possible.

So, when I heard the RN say to run the EKG continuous, I knew what that meant. A serious cardiac issue was taking place. As a nurse was placing the final EKG electrodes on this ladies' chest I looked down at my screen and noticed her heart rate was well over 190 beats per minute. She was in SVT[75] and a medication named Adenosine was about to be administered.

Wait, what the heck did I walk into here?

Ok reader, time to pause.

Let me tell you about this medication. Adenosine is a drug that slows cardiac conduction, way down. Picture a reset button on your WIFI router. You push it and everything powers down and then after a second or two it typically comes back online and resets back to normal. This is what Adenosine does.

Now when you push this drug there are several items you want to have in the room. Chiefly, because there are times when the rhythm doesn't start back up the way you'd like, and you must either shock to cardiovert the rhythm or begin CPR. I've seen this happen.

So, you darn sure better have a crash cart in the room and you want your patient on defib pads so you can shock them should the rhythm come back super funky.

---

[75] Supraventricular tachycardia is an abnormally fast or erratic heartbeat that affects the heart's upper chambers.

Also, make darn sure you have suction on the wall ready to go in the event you need to take over the airway.

As I look around the room I see no crash cart, no LIFEPAK 20 defibrillator to shock the patient, no oxygen cannula in the nose, and no suction hooked up, ready to go.

Failure on all counts.

This startling fact causes me to look around the room and discern who is here.

There are two nurses from the MACU and then the Hospitalist (Admitting doctor for the hospital).

I had to respect their optimism. I mean by all accounts the medical staff were certain that everything was going to work out just fine with this cardioversion. Problem was I came from the ER and we're notorious pessimists. We are certain things will go wrong so we prepare accordingly.

Truth be told I wasn't worried for the patient because I noticed the RN was about to push the medication through a 20 gauge IV in the left hand. The "half-life" of the medication would cause the Adenosine to lose its effectiveness before it reached the heart.

Now, I'm a medic, not an RN and certainly no doctor, so I bit my tongue. I don't want to look like a pompous jackass.

The doctor looks at me and says, "Ok, go ahead and run the continuous EKG."

I reply, "Yes ma'am" and hit the button. The paper begins to pour out the side of the machine as it records the real time rhythm of the heart.

The Doc looks at the RN and says, "Go ahead, push the Adenosine."

The RN repeats the order verbally and then pushes the medication very slowly so as not to burn the patient's hand. She then nonchalantly grabs an IV flush which still needs to be removed from its plastic wrapper. After several seconds she wipes the hub of the port and injects the saline chaser.

Everyone looks at the monitor, but I don't bother. I know nothing's going to happen.

The doctor says, "Hmmm, ok, lets prep to do another dose."

Ok, I can't remain silent any longer. Medic or no, it's obvious these folks are not familiar with this drug.

The trick is to offer advice in a way that makes it sound as if it's the doctor's idea.

So, I take the plunge, "Hey Doc. Since the half-life is so short on this medication how about I get you a large bore IV in the AC[76], hook up a 3-way stopcock direct to the IV catheter, and we then infuse the medication. I'll immediately follow it up with a rapid flush of 30cc of saline. What do you say?"[77]

To her credit the Doc said, "Sure, that sounds like an excellent idea."

She couldn't help herself though and glanced down at my ID badge to see just who the heck I was.

I started a large bore IV in the AC and then hooked up the rest just as I suggested to the doctor.

---

[76] The big vein in the bend of the arm.
[77] I believe the procedure has been updated at the time of this writing. I believe they just infuse into a large bore IV in the AC but straight into an IV line which is hooked up to a bag of saline.

I then explained to the RN, "Ok, you are going to put the syringe of Adenosine on that port, and I'm going to put the saline here on this other one."

I looked up and the RN was smiling. She was having a blast learning something new. She said, "This is so cool. I've never seen this before."

I cringed but didn't say anything knowing the patient must be thinking, "Wait, what the heck did she just say?"

I smiled, put my hand on our patients left shoulder and explained to her, "We got ya. You're in good hands. When the nurse pushes this medication, it's going to make you feel super weird. Other patients I've had report that their chest feels flush for a quick second. It's ok though. That's how it's supposed to feel. Your job is to lay your head back, take deep slow breaths and relax."

I tap the patient's shoulder which brings her attention to me. When she looks me in the eye I confirm, "You good?"

She nods her head. I smile, look over at one of the RNs and say, "When the Doc gives the order just hit that button that indicates 'continuous EKG' right there."

She nods her head.

I now hand the baton back to the doctor, "Ok Doc, ready when you are."

The doctor says, "Go ahead and start the EKG."

The Doc waits a second, ensures the recorded EKG is coming out the side of the machine, looks at the nurse beside me and says, "Administer the Adenosine."

The nurse repeats the order out loud and pushes the medication into the IV. I instantly flip the three-way valve and rapid flush the IV with 30ml of saline and then lift the patients arm up over her head.

We watch the monitor which almost instantly shows a change in rhythm. It flatlines for a second (normal), the patient makes a "woooaaahh" sound and then the rhythm comes back. It's a beautiful normal sinus rhythm. Success!

The nurses were all smiles and talking about how cool it was to do that, "Thank you for coming in here and showing us how to do that."

I said, "Hey no problem. Thank you for being so willing to learn from a lowly medic."

They laughed and rebuffed my playful attempt at debasement.

Out in the hall the doctor asks, "What's your background? Where'd you come from?"

I reply, "Oh yeah Doc, I worked twelve years in a Level One Trauma Center. Ten of those on night shift."

The doctor smiles and says, "Oh, ok, yeah it all makes sense now."

We laughed but inwardly I was worried. I mean if the admitting doctor and nurses are going to be pushing medications, they need to be aware of the risks. The room should have been prepped for a failure.

I ended up talking to my director behind closed doors and she agreed that a report needed to be given the CNO (Chief Nursing Officer) so she could advise the director of the MACU about education on such matters.

I was respectful of the nurses and knew they were compassionate and sharp. I really liked both of them and would often stop by to chat. Having gone through this experience with them made me respect these nurses even more.

Here's why.

They were willing to learn from me, a medic, and that says a lot about their character. They could have viewed me as a "nurses' helper" and dismissed me. However, in me they saw an opportunity to learn from someone who'd been dealing with these sorts of emergencies for a long time. They jumped at the opportunity, no matter whom the instruction came from.

Quite commendable.

Knowing their humility, work ethic, and eagerness to learn I have no doubt their patients of the future will be well taken care of.

For me, it was pleasurable to use my skills to help a patient while also training others, something I'm always passionate about.

A Village

It was a busy day from the minute we clocked in. All of the rooms were full. We even had stretchers in our hallways which was super rare for us. The exam tables in triage were even used to hold patients. Yes, we were getting inventive. I'd have not been surprised to look in housekeeping's closet and find a patient on a stretcher in there.

One of the patients in triage was a homeless guy who stood out to me solely because his shoes were held together by duct tape. The tape, as it was, appeared that it would soon fail.

Seeing his plight an idea took hold in my mind.

I called our chaplain, "Hey this is Dennis in the ER. We've got this homeless fella here who has no shoes. How hard would it be for you to put out the word and get some shoes for this guy? He wears a size eight."

Our chaplain was the best I've ever seen. She fit the mold that I believe God intended. Humble. Graceful. Cheerful. Forthright. Encouraging. Just awesome.

She said, "Let me make some calls. What's our window?"

I laughed, "Well, we're slammed in the ER and it's raining and cold outside, so I imagine he's not leaving any time soon."

"Ok, I'm on it," she said.

One of my nurse buddies walked up to me and said, "Hey Blocker, I heard what you're trying to do, I want to help."

He went to the phone and called his fiancé who was a managing director at a local JC Penny. After telling her the issue she went to the shoe department, picked out a couple pairs, paid for them and then brought them over to the ER.

Meanwhile the chaplain had put her people to work and in a matter of a couple hours a pile of stuff had arrived.

I looked down at the assortment of goods and beamed with satisfaction. There was a new backpack, several pair of warm woolen socks, two pair of brand-new shoes and some house slippers that looked super cozy.

The nurse and I walked up to this fella, and I said, "Sir, while you were lying here a team of people you've never met have been working on your behalf all over the city. Here's what we have for you."

He opened the backpack and tears flowed, "Thank you, thank you so much. Why would you do this for me? Thank you so much."

I gave the guy a man hug, said nothing and departed to carry out my duties.

Throughout the rest of the shift those words kept popping in my mind, "Why would you do this for me?"

A good question.

I can't think of any other reason than, we had to. We just had to do it. It was the right thing to do. Our village had come together to help one of its own.

Saving a Doc

Sepsis is a killer.

There was (and is) a nationwide commitment in healthcare to confront sepsis and protocols were in place. In fact, we even added sepsis to our "Alerts" that were paged overhead. It was taken very seriously then and remains so to this day.

So, what is sepsis?

The CDC describes sepsis as the body's extreme response to an infection. It's a life-threatening medical emergency that happens when an infection you already have, triggers a chain reaction throughout your body. Essentially your body overreacts. Infections that lead to sepsis most often start in the lung, urinary tract, skin, or gastrointestinal tract. Without timely treatment, it can rapidly lead to tissue damage, organ failure, and death.[78]

Yeah, it's no joke.

So, one day I was walking down the hall, avoiding a CPR in progress that they were working in the code room.

---

[78] https://www.cdc.gov/sepsis/what-is-sepsis.html

This avoidance was a behavior I had recently adopted to preserve my sanity. It was sporadic, yes, but definitely a behavior that should have triggered multiple alarms.

It was so uncharacteristic of me. Of course, if I was the only medic on the floor, well then, I'd have to suck it up and work the Code. I'd commit 100% to the task at hand, but if there was another medic on the clock, I'd gladly let them handle the codes. I'd go stock the rooms, IV carts or anything that would keep me from the shadow of death.

On this day there was an additional medic who was eager to work the "CPR in progress" cases so I was ecstatic. He could have them all. However, I did keep my radio volume up on my earbud just in case the team sounded like they were facing some difficulties. In that event I'd jump in quick.

I told myself that the other medic would never learn if I was always doing the tasks. He needed to face the hard things. This is what I told myself anyway.[79]

---

[79] Now understand, these nurses and medics were exceptionally smart and proved themselves over and over again to be proficient at working codes. They could not think of everything though and this is where I came in. Especially when it came time to run equipment like the Rapid Infuser, the Arterial Line monitoring System, CVP monitoring, the LUCAS.

My conscience had other plans though, "Dennis, get your butt over to the Code Room, pop in and make sure they're fine."

Walking down the long hall toward the Code Room I saw a familiar face poke out from one of the side patient treatment rooms. It was a doctor I'd worked with at the Level One Trauma Center.

I smiled, gave her a huge hug, and exclaimed, "Hey Doc! What the heck are you doing here?"

Lisa[80] seemed relieved to see me, "Thank God you're here Dennis. Please come in, I need your help."

I entered the patient room and there on the gurney was her husband, who was also an ER doctor, OURS! Seeing him writhing on the bed and mumbling incoherent phrases kicked me into another mode. This was serious. Sepsis for sure!

I looked up at the monitor and noticed that his blood pressure was tanking, and his heart rate was over 140. He was sweaty, clammy, and thrashing all over the bed. I asked him a question, "Hey Doc! How're you doing! What's going on?"

---

[80] A pseudonym

He looked at me, but his eyes seemed to look through me. Almost as if he was looking at a picture behind me on the wall. Not good.

This was serious! He was dying right in front of my eyes.

Ok, this is unacceptable! I instantly knew we were way behind the treatment window. I couldn't fault the nurse because our septic patient here had been brought to her room while she was in the Code Room. She was pushing resuscitation medications on the cardiac arrest patient.

I looked up to the IV pole where there should have been some IV fluids hanging. There were none. Looking down to his arms and hands I expected to see IV ports that we could infuse IV fluids into. None were there! Crud!

I thought to myself, "Ok Blocker, you're going to have to take over his care right here and now."

I immediately reached down to my large cargo pants pockets and grabbed some IV supplies. I then tried my best to dry off a good spot on his flailing arm, but it was quite difficult. His skin was cold, clammy, and covered with perspiration.

While I worked at a fast clip a concerned Lisa quietly said, "I hated to bother you guys. I know you're working a code in there."

I replied, "My gosh Doc, I wish I had known sooner. I would have popped in here right away."

After locating a good vein, I used an arm holding technique I'd learned when dealing with trippin meth heads. With his arm locked in position I sterilized a good spot, pulled out an 18-gauge IV catheter and was successful on the first poke.

"Impressive," said his wife, "good job. You made that look easy."

I chuckled, "Well Doc, I learned this technique working alongside you over at the Trauma Center. It hasn't failed me."

While I secured the IV port in place Lisa prepped the IV solution and then handed me the fluid line which I connected to the port. I told the Doc, "Open the fluids wide open!"

Lisa did as I asked and then I said, "Hey Doc, that tape is not going to hold. Please watch that line while I go grab some tincture.[81]"

With all the sweating and gyrations, the tape on the IV was already beginning to shake loose.

I grabbed some tincture of benzoin and scrubbed his arm around the IV site. I then secured it in place with an oversized Tegaderm,[82] a flat arm board and then wrapped it all up with some neon green coban tape. Perfect!

In no time at all the first bag of saline was almost completely infused. Then in stepped the nurse who'd been assisting with the CPR in progress. When she saw who our patient was and how critical appeared her whole countenance changed in an instant. I brought her up to speed on everything that had been done.

She called in the ER Doc and some fresh orders were placed.

My shift was soon over but I stopped in to see Lisa and her husband. She was sitting in the dark watching YouTube videos on her phone. I smiled and waved.

---

[81] A sticky substance that works wonders for securing tape to sweaty arms.
[82] A clear and sticky plastic dressing.

She came out into the hallway, huge smile on her face and wrapped her arms around my neck and squeezed me real tight.

"Thank you so much Dennis," she said.

I replied, "I'm so glad I walked by and was able to help."

Peeking into the room I could see that her husband was asleep and resting comfortably. His bed upstairs was ordered, and it would only be a matter of time before he went up.

"It's so nice to see him resting," was my understatement of the year.

I turned and looked to Lisa who was nodding her head and smiling. With that I bid her good night, clocked out, and went home.

Weeks went by and then one day as I was walking up to the clerk to ask a question, I heard a voice exclaim,
"There's the guy that saved my life!"

I turned around and there was our septic Doc, looking amazing. In fact, he was there for a shift with us.

He was beaming as he called out to all the staff, "Hey everyone, see this guy right here! He saved my life!"

The Doc gave me a huge bear hug and exclaimed, "Lisa told me everything that you did for me. Thank you so much Dennis!"

I was taken aback by his words, but I managed to say, "I'm so glad I could help you Doc."

It was such a rewarding moment I'll never forget.

Twins

The radio squelched!

Our heads turned toward it, watching as the Charge Nurse waited for the inevitable report.

"Be advised we are bringing in a twenty-four-year-old woman who just gave birth to twins at a mid-wife facility. The placenta has not come out and she is bleeding profusely. Her systolic is seventy and we cannot register a diastolic pressure. Her heart rate is one fifty-five, I repeat one, five, five. How copy?"

At the end of the report, they estimated their arrival to be two minutes.

I sprinted to the code room and began to set up IV start kits and told the clerk to call the Blood Bank for Crash Blood.

It seemed that seconds later the EMS crew was bursting through our doors, blood drops trailing, marking their path behind them.

This young Hispanic female was completely pale. She had lost all her color to the point that her gums were white as were her nail beds. She was incredibly lethargic and was mumbling, "Tell my babies I love them."

My inner voice was shouting, "Crap! Crap! Crap! This lady has minutes to live!"

On the outside I was a cool cat instructing what we needed.

One of the nurses was trying to start a large bore IV, a 16 gauge. I watched as her hand moved toward the vein. The young RN had heard the plummeting vital signs, had seen the colorless skin, and heard the mumbling drowsy mother speak. As she moved the IV needle toward the vein her hand was violently shaking.

I whispered, "Do you want me to do that?"

She exhaled, "Oh my god, yes please."

I stepped in, grasped the IV catheter and in one motion had a patent line started. As I was taping up the lifeline, I noticed one of the nurses was fumbling with the rapid infuser tubing, having a hard time remembering how to set it up.

I then asked the trembling nurse, "Please finish securing this IV site so we can get that crash blood going."

I stepped to the other side of the young lady and started another sixteen gauge IV on that side. While I did this, I slowly, concisely talked another nurse through the steps of priming the tubing for the rapid infuser.

"Blood Bank's here!" cried a woman standing in the door with an ice chest in her hands.

Soon we had units of blood flowing into this brand-new mother of two beautiful daughters.

Minutes later an OB/GYN doctor was at the bedside. He announced, "They're prepping a room for her now. Let's package her up and get her moving."

We had her ready to go in seconds. As the OR staff surrounded her and whisked her out the door, I was encouraged to see her cheeks had a nice red hue to them and her nail beds were now pink. Our patient was awake, lucid, crying and thanking us for saving her life.

Even now I get tears of joy in my eyes thinking about how we had saved this mother. It was one of the most rewarding days I'd experienced in the ER in a long time. I think of her from time to time and wonder how she and the kiddos are doing. One thing I know, she was able to go home and see them because we had acted expertly, quickly. I'm so grateful for that.

The rest, well that's up to her.

Time to Move On...Again

It was time to leave.

I grew tired of the workload. We were a small hospital, and our facility had not grown with the city. It was getting dangerous for the patients because we didn't have enough space for all the sick folks who were coming in. Nor did we have adequate staff to safely manage the numbers. It was dicey.

For most of my shifts, I was the only Medic on the floor. This of course meant I was leaned on heavily. I was spent. Of course, it was an honor that I was trusted so implicitly, but no one could see what was happening to my heart and spirit.

I'm not sure what my game plan was. I mean, I knew the job was killing me, psychologically, but I couldn't leave it. I needed the money to support my family and it was the only job I knew to do.

I was making too much to quit but not enough to slow down. Does that make sense?

I was drowning. It was like I had a life jacket that would keep me afloat if I kept breathing into a tiny tube. The problem was I was getting exhausted.

I still received commendations and had even won the Hospital Employee of the Month. I had a photo shoot, was given a nice, framed certificate and some gift cards. It was very nice and most appreciated. My work ethic kept me employed and the love for my daughters kept me afloat.

I'm certain that if it were not for those two factors, I would have just walked off the job and never looked back.

But, I kept returning. Kept swallowing that bitter pill. Faced the demons that piled on nightmare after nightmare and sorrow upon grief. All the while praying for a miracle.

Something needed to give so I decided to transfer to the main hospital in our health system. I learned they had seven Medics/ER Techs per shift. I'd no longer be running solo.

Perhaps a change of pace would help. At the very least it would extend my expiration date.

Ups and Downs

Well, it was worth the try but a change in facilities didn't help.

I should clarify this by saying that my new ER definitely added some years to my survivability, but it was only prolonging the inevitable.

This new group of nurses and medics were amazing. I'd never worked with a more efficient team. Daily I was impressed by the team's vigor and drive to complete tasks sooner than later. This group worked hard, and I was to discover they played just as hard on their time off.

Regarding the medics in the ER, I should mention that many were prior military with combat experience.[83] They were predominantly male and were typically eight to fifteen years older than most of the nurses. We looked out for the RNs like kid sisters or daughters in some cases.

My new ER family was a tight knit group that celebrated birthdays together and took tubing trips down the Guadalupe and Comal Rivers. We had dinner parties, get

---

[83] There were a few medics like myself who had no military or combat experience but who had extensive experience in EMS working with Ambulance and Fire Departments.

togethers, movie nights, beach parties, in short, I found a family.

It was the friendship and love that I received from these amazing people that allowed me to eke out a couple more years in Emergency Medicine.

There was one huge difference though. I was the only medic who had worked in a Level One Trauma Center. However, several of the nurses had worked Level One and others had significant experience working critical care patients.

My knowledge was definitely a boon, but I found I was not leaned on as heavily. Still, there were times I'd be the only one on shift with that certain skill set to handle emergent issues.

Working the Intake Desk in triage one day I was surprised to hear one of the nurses call out, "Hey Blocker, they're calling for you in the code room, seems there's an issue with the Level One Rapid Infuser.[84]"

---

[84] This was a machine that squeezed units of blood forcing the life sustaining liquid into the patient at a rapid rate. The bonus for trauma victims was that it also warmed the blood. I grew proficient with this machine from my days at the Level One Trauma Center.

This was serious. If the RNs want to use that piece of equipment it's because there's a patient who needs blood, like, yesterday.

Sprinting down the hall, I turned left into the code room, stepped up to the malfunctioning piece of equipment, placed three fingers on a black latch, pushed up with some force, turned and began to leave the room. The machine kicked on, the alarm silenced, and the infuser purred like a kitten.

As I was leaving one of the nurses exclaimed, "Hey! Wait a minute! You burst in and in less than two seconds you have the machine working! You're just gonna ride off into the sunset aren't you!"

We all laughed and yes, I did fix it that fast and yes, I had to ride off into the sunset because we were getting killed in triage. I needed to get back to the front desk.

Another day I was stocking the code room when a couple nurses whisked in a patient on a stretcher. There was a gaggle of doctors following behind, conversing. I'd never seen these Docs before but the attention they received indicated they were special.

Turns out the patient worked for a prominent physician in the city (Never hurts to name drop if you can). This gentleman had been complaining of a tearing sensation in his chest.

When asked about the pain he replied, "No, I've not been lifting weights or moving heavy objects. The symptoms began when I was driving to work this morning."

The patient had already been taken to CT where images revealed his aorta was dissecting.

The aorta is the main artery that carries blood away from your heart to the rest of the body. It's a large vessel and necessary for life.

Now, for reference, imagine a water hose with a nozzle at the end. Turn the handle on the spigot so that the water enters at full pressure. Now, imagine that the nozzle at the end is closed tight. When you hold the hose, you can feel the strength of the water inside the hose. It has weight and you know it's seeking to burst out.

Well, this guy's aorta was that water hose and unfortunately the layers of the hose were starting to separate. If the final layer is breached, death would be in seconds. The guy was on borrowed time.

His wife and daughter came in to say their goodbyes. It was an emotional moment, but the doctors quickly had them step out so we could prep the patient for his air medical flight to Houston.

Of course, the obvious question is, "Why fly to Houston?" Well, there are very few doctors in the State of Texas qualified to conduct this emergency surgery. Of those few only one was available right then, and he was in Houston.

As you can imagine the room is abuzz with activity as the patient is disrobed, the leads, pulse oximeter and blood pressure cuff affixed, and a game plan discussed.

One of the doctors, the Intensivist[85] from our hospital, spoke to the RN listing several items he would need. She jotted down the list and stated, "Got it." and then the doctor left the room to begin charting.

As the doctor left the room to consult with the collection of other specialists, the RN turned toward me and was pale. Looking down at the list and then up at me she said, "You know you're not leaving this room, right. Because I

---

[85] A board-certified physician who provides special care for critically ill patients. Also known as a critical care physician.

have no idea how to set-up any of the things he just asked for."

Smiling, I said, "Don't worry. I got your back."

First, I set up a small table for the Cordis tray the Intensivist would use to access the femoral vein in the groin. This procedure would place a port through which the patient could be given medications and blood product should the necessity arise.

Then I prepped the Sonosite[86] with a sterile sleeve. This piece of equipment would allow the doctor to view the vessels inside the patient's groin area. The necessity for this procedure centers around the fact that the artery and the vein lie side by side. One pulsates while the other does not. The doctor did not wish to place this large port into the artery, hence the Sonosite machine.

A few seconds later the Intensivist returned to the Code Room. I helped him don his sterile gown and prepare the sterile field across the patient.

As the doctor set about prepping his tray I began to set up and prime the arterial line that would be used to

---

[86] A portable sonogram machine that allows providers to see the vessels inside the body. One could also look at masses, organs and even look at a fetus.

monitor, in real time, the patients blood pressure. To monitor the pressure the doctor would place a small catheter into the patient's radial artery located in the wrist. The catheter is then connected to a small IV line which is married up to a special device called a transducer.

This transducer is then linked to the monitor via a cable which looks very similar to an ethernet line. The blood pressure would then be displayed on the monitor in real time. Such a tool is invaluable for the nurse instantly knows if she needs to increase or decrease the medication pump that is dispensing the blood pressure medication.

After a few minutes all the procedures were completed without a hitch. Everything went smoothly.

The acknowledgment of my work came toward the end when the Intensivist asked my name. Funny how after doing this work for so many years I knew the fact that when someone of that stature asks my name, it's their way of saying "thank you".

Anyway, these were the moments that brought satisfaction. Taking an active part in saving someone's husband, father, and friend. I'd been a huge factor and it felt amazing.

Such victorious moments seemed to be few and far between. Truthfully though, my mind had become clouded to the fact that the abuela (grandmother) I had grabbed a warm blanket for was equally as important and appreciative. My worth was in my work ethic which positively impacted dozens of lives each and every day. It was not just during the extreme cases that I demonstrated my value. My worth was exhibited in the careful and professional way I started an IV. The way I gently placed warm socks on cold feet. The thoughtful dimming of lights so a patient could rest.

My **Dark Passenger** had clouded my mind so deftly regarding my worth, that it was only these extreme cases that brought satisfaction. Now of course when a week later we heard that our aorta patient was doing great, I was thrilled. I knew it was a job well done. However, I should have realized that I had been daily performing such "jobs well done" for years.

Unfortunately, it would be some time before such a realization would finally take hold.

Do I Care?

In these dark days of relentless mental battles, I began to question many things about my life. Was I a good dad? Was I the son that I once was? Do I still care for people the way I used to? Has that part of my soul been hacked away and lost forever?

Two very different people showed me in very dramatic ways that though I was battling some heavy darkness, the Dennis of old was still there.

One shift a message blared over my radio earpiece, "Dennis, can you please go to the Ambulance Bay and see why that lady is banging on the door?"

"Roger that, on my way."

Once outside I was met by a young lady with black streams of old mascara running down her cheeks. She pleaded with me, "Please help my friend. She's not looking too good."

In a beat-up old minivan, I found a young ladies' feet were resting on the front passenger side floorboard. Her waist was wedged between the two bucket seats and her head rested on the backseat, driver's side floorboard. The young lady looked to be about twenty-one years old. She was unconscious but her mouth was open, and half submerged in a pool of vomit. In the van hung a strong aroma of both vomit and alcohol.

She was topless except for tassels which were appropriately placed. She wore a mini skirt and high heels.

I asked her friend, "What the heck happened?"

Her panicking friend stammered with her words. I sensed that she thought she might be in trouble.

I tried to reassure her, "Look, we're not the Cops. I just want to know what happened so we can better take care of her. What you all did is your business."

Her friend said, "Well these doctors were having a party and we got hired to dance for them. We got super drunk, and she fell off the table and split her leg open."

I looked down at the leg and sure enough there was a haggard, disgusting red bandana that one of these "doctors" tied around her wound.

I pulled the bandana aside and was surprised to see a six-inch laceration across her lower leg that was full thickness. I could see bone. Oh man was I furious!

I was a bit miffed when I asked, "Why didn't they call an ambulance?"[87]

The dancer replied, "Well, they didn't want the Police to come, and they knew that if the ambulance showed up, there would be questions."

"Wow," was all I could say.

Instances like this just seemed to really irritate me more and more. The frailty of life was more apparent to me and always on my mind. I could just never imagine treating a young woman like that, no matter her profession.

I managed to get her out of the minivan and into my wheelchair. The only way I could keep her head properly in position was by grasping a hand full of her hair and using it against my left wrist as leverage, thus keeping her airway open. I then shrugged my right shoulder up to my right cheek and used it to compress the transmit button on my radio.

My message said it all, "Bringing in a highly intoxicated young lady with airway issues to bed number five. We're going to need a suction setup and a Doc stat."

---

[87] Reader, during this time I'm untangling this young lady from in between the seats and trying to keep her from inhaling vomit.

Mind you, as I'm leveraging her head for airway issues, and awkwardly shrugging my shoulders to transmit, I'm also trying to push the wheelchair with my right hand. We made it to the room without incident and were able to fix her up. She went home later that day.

There was something about that darn Ambulance Bay that just seemed to bring me the weirdest and most serious cases.

"Dennis, please go to the Ambulance Bay, a lady says her dad is not doing too well."

The call over the earpiece in my ear sent me on the errand yet again.

Arriving in the Ambulance Bay I saw a man slumped over in the front seat. I opened the door and reached up to his neck…no pulse.

I yelled over my shoulder, "Tell them I'm doing CPR in the Ambulance Bay, and I need a stretcher out here!"

The guy had his seatbelt on and who knew how long he'd been without a pulse, so it was vital I start compressions.

The seatbelt was an issue and seemed to be stuck. I told the daughter to get the darn thing off. I pushed against the guy's chest with my right arm as hard as I could, hoping the back of the seat would provide enough resistance so I could get some blood to flow.

Push, push, push, push, push, push.

Sweat poured down my face. My arm's screamed for respite and my back pleaded for mercy. I kept pushing.

The seatbelt was off, but I was still waiting for the stretcher. I shimmied and squeezed into the front a little bit more. I now had a better angle and could more efficiently push on this poor guy's chest. In those prolonged seconds my mind recalled the patient I'd had years before at the Trauma Center, the McDonalds bag between his legs. I'd been doing CPR in the back seat then, now it was the front.

Seconds later the stretcher was there, and we lifted him out and whisked him into the code room.

We worked him for a good thirty minutes before it was determined he was beyond help. There was just nothing we could do.

All that exertion. It was not enough.

You know, the part that really got to me was the grieving of the family. I just hated to hear that. I'd been ignoring it for years. Well, I pretended that I was ignoring it, but sorrow always creeped in a little each time. I thought to myself, "We professionals act like we're pillars of stone, but we care, I care."

Then the realization hit me, "Wait, I care. I do! I actually care! I still have feelings! I'm still human! I have hope! I can still be a human in this life!"

Countdown

It was refreshing to know that the old Dennis was still there and that I cared. The trouble was that I didn't see any light at the end of the tunnel. I was on a treadmill, exerting myself, but to what end?

For weeks I'd been dreading work more than usual, and that is saying quite a lot. My spouse didn't drive so I had the only car in the family. My mother-in-law, at the time, asked if she could use my car to take the kids to school and pick them up every day. This meant that I would have to find my own way to work every shift, which of course required me to ask friends for a carpool to and from work. Most times though, I was to discover it would come down to an Uber ride.

I could only think, "When dad was my age he had a house, two cars, retirement from the military, a second career and here I am bumming rides to work."

I felt worthless and was in a major funk.

For months I'd been having nightmares and my girls had instructions to wake me if they heard me yelling. My hope was that they'd pull me out.

This worked like a charm. Several times Lauren, my oldest, would roll me side to side saying, "Daddy wake up! Daddy, wake up! You're yelling."

I asked Lauren, "What did I say baby?"

She replied, "It wasn't words, it was just yelling."

My nightmares typically featured children with horrendous wounds bleeding out and crying. However, occasionally the ten-year-old blonde girl with the dog bite to the neck would visit me. She never said a word. She just stood among oily darkness, as she glowed white. These nightmares were on a loop.

Things were breaking down at home. I felt utterly alone.

There were many days I couldn't afford Uber rides home. I'd have to walk. The trek took me one hour and forty-five minutes.

Here I'm forty-five, walking home in the Texas summer heat, sweating like a boxer. Cars pass me by. I can see the air-conditioning blow their hair as they laugh and chat with friends while sipping iced mochas. Sweat pours down the middle of my back and my feet are aching after walking for twelve hours on shift and now walking home for two.

I had a lot of time to think, "So this is my life. I can't sleep because of nightmares. I bum rides to work and walk home. After twenty-two years in the ER, I'm making just over sixteen dollars an hour. I'm stuck in a career that is killing me. Is this my future? Will a sixty-year-old Dennis be doing this same thing over and over?"

Then came the event that brought everything crashing down.

I was walking down the hallway toward the doors that led out of the ER to the elevator banks. I heard a voice on the radio say, "Can someone check the restroom by bed thirty-one. The call light is going off."

I hopped on the radio, "This is Blocker, I'll check it out."

I walked to the restroom, knocked and said, "Can I help you. This is Dennis, I'm one of the medics here."

A faint female voice called out, "Yes, please come in, I need some help."

The door was locked but there's a feature on the knob that allows us to flip a switch and unlock the door for just such a situation.

I flipped the switch, gently opened the door, and called out, "Hello this is Dennis, one of the medics, are you okay?"

There was a lady sitting on the toilet. Her pants were on the ground. She had tears in her eyes as she said, "I think I had a miscarriage."

I said, "Ok ma'am, let me help you."

I walked toward her, put my right hand gently on her shoulder and said, "To your right is a rail. Grasp it and use it to maintain your balance. I need you to stand a little so I can see what's going on."

The lady stood just a tad allowing me to look down into the toilet bowl.

There in the toilet water, blood, and clots lay a fully developed baby connected to an umbilical cord. This baby had undergone at least six months gestation and had tiny, beautiful little arms, legs, and facial features.

The baby was obviously dead. I looked down at the little life floating in that porcelain bowl that had received thousands of bowel movements. My mind momentarily went blank, but I recovered quickly.

I told the lady, "Ok, go ahead and sit down. I'll get some nurses to help you."

I picked up my radio, "I need some nurses to come to the restroom now."

The rest is kind of a blur. I know that at one point I scooped the baby, the umbilical cord, and placenta out and placed it in a bucket I'd retrieved from the lab.

The rest is hazy.

I seemed to wander the hallways for a bit. My next memory is my charge nurse Alexa asking me, "Dennis, are you ok?"

I couldn't act anymore. It was time to turn in my "Screen Actors Guild" credentials. I wasn't going to lie one single day more. NOT ONE MORE!

I said, "No, I'm not ok."

I burst into tears and walked toward the back of the ER exiting outside. Sitting on a stone wall I was soon surrounded by several nurses including Alexa and Damaris (both Charge Nurses) who were holding me as I sobbed and sobbed. I kept repeating, "I can't do it anymore. I can't do it anymore."

Soon a couple more nurses came to my side and the huddle squeezed in on me. I'll always be grateful for them.

Alexa stayed with me for a while and said, "I want you to go home. Take the rest of the day off."

I clocked out and stepped into the free world. Across the street was the park and beautiful trees that I'd sat under at lunch time. There was the trail that I'd walked contemplating my future. My mind wondered, "How am I going to survive this?"

Then, I walked home for I couldn't afford an Uber.

I didn't know it then but that baby in the toilet speeded up a countdown that had been ticking for years. My time in the ER was limited.

I couldn't stand the idea of working there anymore.

Did I love my coworkers?

Absolutely!

Did I love taking care of sick people and making them better?

Without question, YES!

So, what was the problem?

I was tired of the company of my **Dark Passenger.** I was weary of his stench. I despised his depressive stories that he'd tell me in quiet moments.

This was a huge problem for my unwanted companion was a voracious storyteller. I mean he wouldn't shut up and he followed me everywhere. Church. The Mall. The Movie Theater. The Book Store. Restaurants. The Beach. Birthday Parties. Christmas. Basketball Games. Music Concerts. Camping. Fishing.

My **Dark Passenger** was the worst nagging companion a guy ever had, "Oh, see that smiling girl over there wearing that shirt with the word 'PINK' on the front? My, my, my, that reminds me of that fifteen-year-old girl who was run over by an SUV when she was out jogging. You remember her, don't you Dennis?"

The **Dark Passenger** massages my brain and purrs, "Remember how the earbuds were forced into her skull? Recall that big hole she had in her cranium from her head bouncing off the pavement and then against the underside of the truck when it ran over her?"

The **Dark Passenger** loves to remind me of that one because there's so many articles of clothing sporting that innocuous word. PINK.

I shake my head like an Etch-o-Sketch hoping it will erase the memory but it's too late and my companion knows it. He won't be happy until my face contorts into a snarled grimace of nausea. He needs acknowledgement.

Now that I'm immersed into his story he says, "Well, perhaps you'll see something like that again today at work. What do you think?"

My brain races for an escape but there's nothing I can do.

Each morning I'd punch my arms through the provided holes in my scrub top. I'd slip on those raggedy old scrub bottoms and wear the same old nasty tennis shoes. I didn't even take them inside the house anymore for they have the odor of the **Dark Passenger** on them. I hate him…and my shoes.

I snatch up my phone, plug in the information for my Uber ride and as I await the pickup, I don my headphones and seek to drown out his creaky voice.

I settle on some Viking war chant music by Heilung because the thought of listening to something cheerful or hopeful makes me sick to my stomach.

As I step into the vehicle a snarl crosses my face. I confirm the address and hope I never have to talk to this happy, caffeinated driver again. He revolts me. I bet he has a better companion.

The closer I get to the hospital the tighter the knot in my belly gets. I feel like there's an octopus in my stomach wrapping its tentacles around my guts.

The driver says something about the kind of day he hopes I have, and I step out into the free world. A few more seconds of fresh air before the plunge back into the world of no windows, bleak painted walls and overhead lights that seem to suck the life force out of me.

Passing hospital workers, patients, and their families I look straight ahead, music blaring in my top tier headphones. Unrecognizing anyone. It's the way I want it.

My last chance to turn around comes at the time clock, but I dutifully swipe my badge for I have children to provide for. I must do the right thing even if it kills me.

Day after day, the same routine.

"Oh, Dennis, hey that lady there. She reminds me of someone," says the **Dark Passenger**.

I try to avoid thinking about it, but he is of course persistent, "Ah yes, I remember now…remember that teenager you and the team tried to save?"

The **Dark Passenger** smiles because he knows that he's not provided enough information. He gets me and understands that this old trick always reals me in. I'll require a bit more detail for there have been so many dead teens through the years and he's only too glad to provide the background.

"It was graduation night for the majority of high schools across the city," hisses my putrid sidekick.

The venomous words penetrate my memory banks and project the scene onto my mind's eye in Technicolor.

He has me yet again, "Do you recall that this young man had no identification on him? The kid hung upside down by his seatbelt. Remember that?"

Of course, I remember but I don't let on that I do.

I instantly regret it because if I had at least acknowledged the memory perhaps he would have moved on. In my stubbornness I've made it worse, and he revels in my old, tired mistakes.

He spews out the details, "As I recall didn't a lady show up at the front desk asking if the ER had received a young man fitting a description she provided?"

Before I could acknowledge the story this snake of a storyteller pushes on, "She looked nice, didn't she? I could see she was a good mom and very concerned for her boy who'd not come home when he said he would. Poor lady. Poor, poor, lady."

"I know you remember when the Trauma Resident requested you to go into the private family waiting room and ask the mom for a photo."

The raconteur's musty old breath puffs against my cheek, "I remember the scene well. You did your best to console her but, in the end, you had to admit that there in fact was an unidentified young man who'd come in and had since died. In fact, you knew he was dead before arrival to the ER, but you didn't tell her that because you're such a sweet guy and besides you weren't even sure it was her kid."

Fully invested in the tale I'm a prisoner to his purposes, "Remember walking beside her to the room to see if this was indeed her son? You noticed that the housekeeper, who'd cleaned all the blood off the floor, pulled the curtain shut but had inadvertently pulled too much thus revealing the boy's head to those in the hallway."

Placing his arm across my shoulder the **Dark Passenger** took me there, "When you saw his head from the hall, you hoped that you could distract her before she noticed. A split second later there was that shrill, piercing scream that caused you to jump and temporarily deafened your right ear."

"I recall that she screamed that hopeless guttural, animalistic scream that caused the entire ER to fall silent."

Then the **Dark Passenger** begins to mock me, "It's a good thing you were standing there Dennis because she fainted, and you caught her. At an odd angle, you guided her to the ground. You held her tight and rested her head on your shoulder. When she came too, she screamed again into your ringing ear and you held each other, sitting on the floor in the hallway. Rocking. I'll never forget that scene Dennis…the two of you there. Her sobbing on your shoulder and you just squeezing her so tightly. Very touching indeed."

As the poisonous words are uttered, they immediately trigger the memories, I'm right there again.

These scenes were replayed over and over again, day after day, night after night, nightmare after nightmare.

The characters changed.

The settings changed.

I was changed.

I needed a lifeline.

The Shrink

I worked for some amazing people in that, my final, Emergency Department. Most ERs are matriarchal in their administration and ours was no different. These were some of the hardest working, kind, battletested and intelligent nurses I'd ever worked with. Somehow, they had managed to remain compassionate amidst the turmoil.

The same was true of our Charge Nurses[88] who were attentive to the needs of our patients but also their staff.

One morning our Charge Nurse Damaris saw me stocking the Code Room, preparing for the shift. She compassionately asked, "How are you doing Blocker?"

I wasn't good. I'd not been the same since the baby in the toilet and she knew all about that for she'd been one of the nurses holding me as I wept that day.

I replied, "I'm feeling aggressive."

---

[88] I recall one day a Student Nurse had to shadow one of our amazing Charge Nurses for twelve hours. At the end of an exhausting day as he was preparing to leave I said, "Hey man." He looked up at me. I pointed to the Charge Nurse and said, "What do you think about everything she handled today?" He was stunned, "I can't believe how much she did and that she never even seemed concerned or frazzled." I smiled and said, "Just think, all that she handled today and the hospital, to show its appreciation gave her twelve bucks." The student was floored. I continued, "That's right. She makes one dollar more an hour to do what she does, that's it." Incredible.

Damaris put her hand on my shoulder and said, "Go home, take the rest of the day off. Get some rest. Is there someone you can talk to?"

I lied, "Yes, there's someone."

I knew I wasn't going to talk to anyone about it. I was in a seriously dark place, and I couldn't stand the thought of light being shown on my problem.

My Charge Nurses and Director had a different idea though.

My next shift I was called in to the office to chat with my director. There was no wiggle room in what she said to me, "Dennis, go talk to your doctor now."

I had my orders. "Yes ma'am," was my reply.

She'd been doing the job just as long as I had and was not buying my crap, "No Dennis. I'm serious. You're going right now."

One of the assistant directors was called in and instructed, "Please take Dennis to his doctor."

Within minutes I was walking up to the reception desk at my busy clinic. I was done with the struggle, "Ma'am, I don't have an appointment. I work in a local Emergency Room and have been doing the job for over two decades. I'm having some serious PTSD issues and I'm afraid of what might happen if I don't get some help immediately."

The receptionist was amazing. She nodded her head and said, "I'll squeeze you in right away."

I was candid and held nothing back. My doctor had tears in her eyes as I retold some of the stories, the nightmares and what was happening to me. Prescriptions were written and referrals made.

It was because of these amazing people that I was introduced to "The Shrink."

Now, of course this was not how she was referred to me nor how she referred to herself. In my own mind she held this name for I was very skeptical of her knowledge and ability to help me. Her actual name is Elisa Medellin.

When I stepped into Ms. Medellin's office I was in a foul mood. I thought, "How is this book worm gonna help me? She'll never understand what it's like to see what I've seen."

I sat down and she began, "Mr. Blocker, my job on this first day is to see if you qualify for this program. This is reason I had you fill out that long questionnaire. However, before I look at that I want to talk with you."

I said nothing, just blinked and let her steer the conversation.

Ms. Medellin continued, "I want you to tell me about some of the things you've seen that really bother you. You can tell me anything you want."

I held nothing back, "Well, one of the things that really bothers me is the fact that one of my patients ate her own baby."

I went on and on, describing many of the things I'd witnessed.

The counselor said, "Which is the ONE case that really bothers you?"

I said, "It was a two-year-old. She stands out to me because I had to keep her brains from coming out of her skull."

I went on to explain the setting and how I had to prep her body for viewing.

Ms. Medellin sat back in her chair and after I was finished said, "Mr. Blocker, frankly, I've spoken with many combat veterans, and they complain how irritated they get with civilians because they don't understand what they've seen."

She paused to see if I was tracking.

I was, so she continued, "I can tell you that most of the veterans I've spoken with have not seen anywhere near as much of the trauma as you have. I would say it's a certainty that you will qualify for this program. I'll put in the paperwork and contact you when our meetings will begin. Are Wednesdays good for you?"

I replied, "Yes ma'am, Wednesdays are fine."

Though I was guarded and skeptical Ms. Medellin had challenged my mind. I was going to take a chance and see what she had to say. I owed it to my girls to get better.

The following Wednesday was my first official session with my counselor. I was working this day, but I was fortunate on two counts: One, Ms. Medellin's office was across the street from my ER. Two, my director wanted me to heal so she permitted me to clock out and attend the hour-long session.

Anxious and irritable I sat in the chair. My situation was unchanged, and I could see no end in sight. I was doomed. Well, at least that's how it seemed.

Sitting across from me, Ms. Medellin handed me a few sheets of paper to insert into a binder she'd asked me to bring. This would be homework. We talked about what the sessions would look like and what she was hoping I'd do with my assignment.

At one point she said, "Dennis, I can tell you that at some point you're going to get angry and really hate this. We have had a lot of success with this new program, and I truly believe that if you will follow it through, you'll start to heal."

I was skeptical but promised her I would do my best.

She then said, "I want you to write at least one page about that one traumatic event that stands out in your mind. Write how this event made you feel about yourself, others, and the world in the areas of safety, trust, power/control, esteem, and intimacy. Please bring this assignment with you next Wednesday."

I was extremely doubtful that I'd be able to even compose a single page, but I promised I'd do my best.

Dear reader, what follows are the unedited answers I provided to Ms. Medellin. These are some very personal thoughts that I'm sharing. I'm revealing these because they perfectly disclose my mindset. I know there are folks out there who are deeply stuck in the morass of darkness just as I was. I hope that my transparency will encourage you to be honest with yourself and seek the help that you need and deserve.

Consider the Effects this Traumatic Event has had on Belief about Yourself, Others, and the World

1) How did this event effect your beliefs about yourself?

"At first I was surprised that I could witness such events and still perform my job. I found that I could see such horrible things and still function. Truthfully this was a nice surprise because in Emergency Medicine one never knows if you have what it takes until you are in the mix. I was pleased to discover I could hack it. However, I found myself thinking about this toddler quite often and even found her obituary in the

newspaper and cut it out and taped it into a journal I was keeping at the time."

2) How did this event effect your beliefs about others?

"This was a wake-up call to me in that was shown that there are people out there who care nothing for how their decisions impact others. It showed me the cumulative wrath of bad decisions: A) the drunk driver who decided to drive. B) the parents who did not put their daughter in a seat belt. This was my first time I began to hate[89] drunk drivers."

3) How did this event effect your beliefs about the world regarding:

a. Safety

"I was acutely aware that the world is a very dangerous place and whether you seek it out or not death is around every corner just waiting for the opportunity to snatch up a life. To my interactions with my children this has manifested itself in not allowing them to ride jet

---

[89] The word "hate" is underlined twice in my journal.

323

skis, 4 wheelers, ride with other people, visit school buddies homes or play in swimming pools without a life jacket even though the water is very shallow."

b. Trust

"I assume that everyone has an angle and that no one can be trusted at face value. Whereas before I assumed that everyone has good intentions my exposure to these events made me believe that everyone will look to themselves first. Only family can be trusted and then only immediate family."

c. Power/Control

"I never really put much thought into this subject. I assume that folks look for themselves first. Regarding the exertion of power by patients, those seeking to intimidate staff I have adopted a confrontational attitude being sure not to appear weak. I desire to be a sheepdog, not a sheep, nor a wolf. A sheepdog suits me."

d. Esteem

"Intellectually I know that I have accomplished quite a lot and that I have saved thousands of lives and positively touched just as many. However, I feel that I could have done more, could be more, make more money. I feel like a failure, not a success. Once again intellectually I know I have accomplished a lot but yet the "feeling" is there."

e. Intimacy

"Would be nice but it not a reality. It is a fanciful notion appropriate for those in their teens and twenties and for those who watch Hallmark Channel. Reality is it wears off. I long for it but it takes two."

So, I guess you have seen my doubts about filling a single page were misguided. My composition was three pages, handwritten.

On my next session Ms. Medellin was going to dig into what she called "Stuck Points."

Here is the definition of "Stuck Point" from the sheet she handed me, "Stuck points are thoughts that you have that keep you stuck from recovering."

She explained to me that Stuck Points are often formatted in a, "If… / then…" structure. In other words, "If I let others get close, then I will get hurt."

Ok, easy enough.

Ms. Medellin then asked me to read aloud the three-page composition I'd written. After I read aloud the entire composition we went through it again, but this time slowly, stopping when she indicated.

Her purpose was to find stuck points I had unknowingly jotted down in my composition. When Ms. Medellin revealed them to me, I'd write them down on a sheet titled, "Stuck Point Log."

Brilliant.

A few minutes later we finished, and I looked down at the log. Ms. Medellin asked, "Dennis, how many stuck points do you have listed?"

I began to count and replied, "Twenty-five ma'am."

Dear reader, let me put that down again for you. I had twenty-five stuck points festering in my brain from that one little girl.

Here's a couple examples of these stuck points that I had written in my composition:

"It's not fair."

"People don't care how their decisions impact others."

"If she had been buckled up, she would have lived."

Regarding the first example she asked, "Where did you learn the concept that life is fair?"

My brain came to a screeching halt.

I had to be honest, so I answered, "It's not reality. I know that. The real world is hard, and things just happen. I know that life is not fair. To be fair God would have to take away our gift of free will and make us do this, or say that, or make such and such decisions."

Ms. Medellin, with a knowing smile asked, "So is that stuck point based on reality or is it based more on emotions?"

Yeah, she was right. This was going to be hard. She was making me look very closely at myself and the things I had come to believe.

I replied, "It's based solely on emotions and not reality."

We then moved to the next point, but I jumped ahead of her, "Yes, I already see that the second one is totally based on emotions because I know that statement is a flat out lie. Total emotions."

She smiled.

Then came the third one, *"If she had been buckled up she would have lived."*

Ms. Medellin inquired, "Let me ask you, how do you know that she would have lived had the seatbelt been on?"

She let that sink in and continued, "For that matter, how do you know that later that day she might not have died crossing the street and getting hit by a car. What if she died the following day by falling from a window? How do you know she would have lived a long life?"

It was amazing. I could feel weight drop from my shoulders. Reality was I didn't know squat! I didn't know if she was going to later die of cancer or perhaps die in a drowning accident at the beach the following week. I had been carrying around this "Stuck Point" for years and it wasn't based on facts. It was impossible for me to know if she would have lived with the seat belt on. Yet, I carried around that friggin stuck point all those years.

We went through those points one after another. The exercise caused us to exceed the allotted time a bit, but I found this session to be transformational.

I'd been holding on to these thoughts, beliefs, and emotions for years and years. For the first time in a very long time, I began to see some light. I could feel the **Dark Passenger** shudder as his grip on my mind began to weaken.

I felt better, indeed, but I was walking straight back into the Emergency Department to clock in and finish nine more hours of my shift. It was like being cured of a disease but then going right back into the place where you contracted it. Something had to change. But how? When? I was given the tools to process these events properly, and now I needed to seriously think about a career change.

Later that night at home I wondered what the next sessions with Ms. Medellin would bring? Twenty-five stuck points and that was from one little girl! The realization hit me hard for I'd been doing this work for over two decades. The fact that I'd seen hundreds of people die made me wonder how many stuck points were jammed into my brain? Was it thousands? I didn't know, but I now had a strategy to begin dealing with them.

So, about that career change. That was easier said than done. I had a ton to contemplate, but also nothing to fall back on for I had no other line of work that I could do. Well, at least nothing that would keep me at my current pay rate.

So, I dutifully pressed on. Day after day, I approached that evil time clock and obediently slid my ID badge for a good dad does such things.

The countdown to my inevitable final day continued whether I liked it or not, but fate had arranged a meeting with someone I was required to meet.

Cross Country

My spirit had deteriorated considerably. I couldn't bear the beeping of the monitors, and the alarming of the pulse oximeters grated on my sanity. My brain was constantly flashing messages of doubt, failure, and doom. Though Ms. Medellin had given me strategies to deal with my past issues, the problem was my submersion in this environment of pain and suffering.

The previous week my doctor told me that my job was a "Golden Coffin." It was golden because it provided everything I needed for my family. It was a coffin because it was going to kill me.

My doctor looked at me and said, "Dennis, you need to get out of there. You have to do something else."

She was correct but I had no other training. I could not bear the thought of beginning a new job at minimum wage, taking orders from someone right out of high school.

So, to help quiet my mind I had taken to listening to audio books at work. I'd wear a black earbud on the same side as my hospital radio earpiece, thus obscuring it from view. I kept the audiobook volume down and my work radio volume up so when a transmission was made, I'd hear it clearly.

It really helped. I was able to complete all my tasks, start IVs and anything else required, all while listening to amazing stories that prevented my mind from wandering or stalling.

I listened to *The Splendid and the Vile* by Erik Larson, *In the Kingdom of Ice* by Hampton Sides, *Isaac's Storm* by Erik Larson, *Longitude* by Dava Sobel and many other amazing books.

Those authors really helped me cope.

So, anyway, one day I was stocking an IV cart when I heard one of the clerks on the radio ask, "Hey, there's an RV parked in the Ambulance Bay, can someone go out there and see if they need help?"

I answered, "Roger that, this is Dennis. I'm on it."

Walking toward the Ambulance Bay I was soon joined by Alexa our Charge Nurse for the shift.

Sure enough, there was a very large tan colored RV set on the fringe of the Ambulance parking area. I looked and noticed the plates were from California.

A kindly looking tall, lanky fella emerged from the side door of the RV. He looked to be in his early sixties. He had long hair which appeared as if it had not seen a brush in a while. There was something else. His eyes. They looked very tired, very care worn.

I recognized that expression for I'd seen it in my mirror.

We shake hands and Alexa asks, "Do you need some help sir?"

The fella leans back, takes in a deep breath, and tells his story.

So, turns out, in the RV was a dear friend of his. The lady was the same age as he, but she had terminal cancer. This gentleman knew that his best friend only had days, perhaps weeks to live and he would not let her die in a bed, with the shades drawn. He wanted her to see the States. She liked the idea so off they went.

They made it through Arizona, New Mexico and the long eight-hour drive from El Paso to San Antonio when she started to deteriorate quickly. He was worried so he stopped in to see us.

"She's not happy that I brought her here. She doesn't want anything to do with hospitals. You understand, I'm sure. She's tired of being poked," was his warning.

I nodded and replied, "Well, let's go talk to her and see how she's doing."

The fella opened the side door for me, and I stepped up and in. I was immediately assaulted by the heavy odor of urine. This was obviously not a new smell to me, but it did speak volumes. I made my way to her side and gently placed my hand on her right shoulder.

I noticed that the driver had built a platform of wood that rested atop the two benches of what would have been a dinner table. A mattress was then placed on this wooden frame and a rail fashioned on the side, so she'd not topple out. Her immediate view was a large bay window through which she saw the beautiful deserts of Arizona, New Mexico, and Texas.

I was super impressed with this guy and could only hope that in my later days I'd have friends as close to me.

I gently touched this lady's shoulder and said, "Hello ma'am, my name is Dennis. I'm one of the medics here at the Emergency Room. You're here in San Antonio, Texas and your friend has told us about your journey and your situation."

Her eyes were hollow, and I could plainly see the outline of her skull, but she was looking at me, following my conversation. She had days to live. In my gut I knew it to be true.

This was no time for bull crap, so I continued, "Ma'am we know the reality of your situation. You and I know that if you come in the hospital, we're not going to cure you. I know you don't want to come in, but I can tell you that if you do, we can get you an IV and some medications that will allow you to continue on your journey."

She had tears in her eyes, and she nodded her head.

I asked one more time, just to be sure she understood, "Ma'am, will you let me put an IV in you so we can get you some fluids and buy you a little more time for your trip?"

She nodded her head again.

I didn't have gloves but there was no way I was leaving her side. I reached under her frail, emaciated body and my arms were immediately soaked in her urine. I lifted her up very slowly and brought her up close to my chest resting her limp head on my shoulder.

Gingerly I walked through the RV and then negotiated the steps. Alexa had brought out a stretcher with a pillow and blanket on it. I laid her on the mattress with extreme care. We covered her with a blanket and took her into the code room to begin buying her more time.

I'm really proud of that moment. I was proud to have met that fella who loved his friend so much that he would build her a viewing stand for an epic journey across the country. She was going to die her way. Not lying in a dark room but traveling, seeing the country.

I was glad that I had seen this for it proved many of my "Stuck Points" wrong. There **are** people out there who genuinely care about what happens to other people.

My **Dark Passenger** had twisted my mind to the point it was hard to see the good out there. Ms. Medellin had punched through those first layers of that **oily black darkness** and then I had been fortunate to meet this man and his best friend.

Something else happened though. I was reminded that life is precious but it's also sometimes shorter than we'd like.

How long would I stay in this environment? A change needed to happen.

Broken Glass

For weeks I'd been taking my lunches outside under the trees in the park across from our hospital. I just couldn't bear eating in a windowless room. I needed to breath. I'd sit in the grass, close my eyes, feel the wind on my cheeks and run my hands slowly over the grass, trying to feel each and every blade.

I'd tell myself, "Slow breaths, deep breaths. Eyes closed. Music peaceful on the headphones. Go to another place. Leave the sick, the dying behind for thirty minutes. Think about your favorite place, Alaska. Picture yourself on a mountain top overlooking Hatcher's Pass. Feel that cool Alaska air on your cheek. Escape. Relax. Breathe. Feel the grass under your fingers. Feel the life there."

These lunches were a Band-Aid on a huge problem. They only prolonged my time in the ER. They didn't fix the larger issues inside my brain.

My psychiatrist Dr. Davis[90] recommended that I "ground" myself. Following her advice, I took to running my right hand along the walls of the corridors as I walked through the hospital.

---
[90] A pseudonym

I was never one to go for any of that "hippie" stuff, but I thought, "Well, what I've been doing is obviously not working, so I'll try it."

Crazy, but it really seemed to help.

Once again though, it was only a temporary fix to a serious problem.

I was still having nightmares. Now I know they stemmed from the fact that my subconscious knew I was going to head back to the ER in the morning for my shift.

Uber rides, carpools, and walking home were still my common daily modes of transportation to and from work.

Audio books helped keep my mind busy during shifts.

I had no refuge at home.

The light of my life, my girls, were oblivious to the darkness I was in. Well, that's not completely true because Lauren would wake me from my nightmares.

Day after day I was breaking down and I was accepting any opportunity to leave work early which meant my pay was less. I'd walk in the park and let the tears fall. Then I'd step into my home and smile, hug my girls, get their baths done, brush their hair, get them tucked into bed, say their prayers with them, kisses all around and then blowing kisses from the door. My short time with happiness ended the same way every night at their door.

Then, I'd walk to my room where my bed set like a demonic figure, beckoning me to sleep, but then torturing my mind all night long.

Thus, my last day at the Emergency Department began just like all the others. Awake at 5:45 unrested. Order an Uber ride. Listen to my Viking music and stare out the door at the thousands of people with hope.

I was tired. Very tired. Even my soul was exhausted and as the Uber passed by University Hospital, I looked up at their new parking garage and a thought slipped into my brain, "You know, if you step off the top of that thing, your brain will finally shut up."

The thought instantly terrified me because it made sense, "Yes, I'd finally be at rest."

However, the vision of my girls popped into my brain, and I shook the thought of that friggin parking garage out of my head.

Walking toward the time clock I felt nausea welling up inside me, but I dutifully swiped my badge and made my way to the breakroom for our morning "Stand-up."[91]

My name was called out, "Dennis, you're in the triage window today."

I said nothing, just shook my head in acknowledgement.

Sitting at the desk I logged in, sanitized my chair and the counters, made sure my gloves were handy and began to check emails.

Within a short time, it was obvious that this was going to be another busy day. Folks were pouring in one after another. I listened to their Chief Complaint, asked questions that years of experience had trained me to ask, and kept the nurses informed on those I thought were "sicker" than the others.

The line of folks waiting to check in was soon going out into the hallway. To make matters worse we were short staffed so there was no medic assigned to triage to start IVs and send labs.

---

[91] Briefing in which new protocols were discussed by the Charge Nurse. Assignments were given out to the various teams.

My name was said on the radio. It was the Charge Nurse, "Dennis, I'm going to have you start getting the labs up there. I'll replace you with one of the nurses."

I was irritated but I responded with a quick, "Roger that."

In the triage lab station, I called patient after patient and could not successfully start an IV to save my life. I was sticking people two or three times and then sending them back out into the waiting area with an apology and a, "They'll have to get your line once you get in the back."

I was so frustrated at myself because I was proud of my ability to get an IV on the first attempt. We even had a competition going. One shift I was 30 for 30 but that was in the past. Today I was 0 for 6 and I had ten hours of my shift remaining.

"Triage what is the hold-up on getting those labs sent. How come we are not getting results posted from the lab?"

The voice was the Charge Nurse and her question, though valid and appropriate, sparked fierce anger in me.

I didn't reply. I let the question hang in the air.

My next patient I poked and was able to at least get blood, but I couldn't get the darn IV catheter to advance into the vein, so I had to pull it out.

I told the guy, "Well, I'll at least get your labs cooking. Have a seat out front, listen for your name and once you get to the back, they'll get your IV started."

The kindly gentleman nodded his head, thanked me, and stepped out to the waiting area.

I was pissed off. 0 for 7 on my IV attempts and all the while the Charge Nurse calling out to me in my ear, "Where's those labs?"

My **Dark Passenger** slid his arm around my shoulder and laughed.

I logged into our lab software and the computer program stopped running. I restarted the computer and while I waited, I tried using a handheld device to perform the same function, but it wouldn't connect to the internet. My anger and frustration kept mounting and the **Dark Passenger** began heckling me. I was losing control.

Trying a different handheld device, I clicked the button to wake it up and discovered that the battery was dead. I looked over at the battery charging station and it was empty.

"Ha! Ha! Ha! You're useless!" chided my unwanted company.

My hands were shaking, my pulse racing and in my ear, "Triage, once again, what's the hold-up with those labs?"

Finally, with the desktop computer reboot complete, I logged in. Darkness was encroaching on my field of vision making it smaller and smaller. I took the mouse, placed the cursor on the lab program, clicked it twice, and the program crashed.

Instantly the computer screen had a huge crack, and it went tumbling off the side of the countertop. I stared at it as it swung upside down by the power cord. My right fist began to burn. I immediately felt tremendous guilt. I couldn't believe I'd just done that. I punched a computer screen.

I lifted the monitor back onto the tabletop and looked around. No one had seen my disgraceful outburst.

Just then one of the medics popped in, saw the monitor and said, "Hey they sent me up here to help you with... Whoa! What happened?"

I flatly said, "I punched it."

He laughed and then after a few awkward seconds said, "Well, just say that it fell."

I shook my head and said, "No, I'm not going down that road. I'm gonna go talk to the boss."

I knew my career in Emergency Medicine was over.

Walking to her office I can't recall if anyone called out to me, asked me a question or what. I was oblivious to everything around me.

I knocked on her door.

"Come in," came a faint call.

I stepped in, sat down and said, "I just punched the computer screen in the lab station in triage. It's broken."

After a long pause I said, "I can't do this anymore."

The Assistant Director said, "Come on, let's go see Mary.[92]

---

[92] A pseudonym

Mary was our director and someone who always had the best of her staff in mind.

Sitting across from Mary at her desk, the Assistant Director stepped in, closed the door, and sat down beside me.

I looked at my director and said, "Boss, I punched the computer screen in triage. It's broken. Please take the cost out of my check."

Mary looked at me and without missing a beat asked, "How's your hand?"

I replied, "It's ok."

She then asked, "How are you?"

Tears began to fall down my cheeks and I said, "Boss, I can't do this anymore. I just can't. I'm scared because this is all I know to do."

Mary looked at the Assistant Director and said, "Go and find Trent[93] and ask him to come in here please."

---

[93] A Pseudonym

Trent was the hospitals liaison with all of the Emergency Services across the city. He was also someone I'd known on a personal level for over a decade. I was glad she had asked for him to come over.

When Trent entered the room Mary said, "Can you please take Dennis to his doctor?"

He could tell by the energy in the room that something significant had gone down.

Without hesitation he replied, "Absolutely."

Mary looked at me and said, "Dennis go with Trent and see your doctor. We'll talk about all of this later. First though, go see your Doc."

I managed to say, "Yes ma'am."

That was it. I never went back. When I clocked out that day, it was my last time swiping a time clock for Emergency Medicine.

Reviewing my journal that I kept twenty-two years before I see a young man ready to make a difference. I was excited about every opportunity to help people and eager for knowledge.

The end was a broken, weathered, tried, true, battered, dark, fearful, resigned, wizened, and tempered old veteran of the line. I had no idea what the future held but I was determined to be there for my girls. I had to keep fighting for myself and for them.

I guess you could say this was the lowest day of my life and the future appeared very bleak. I knew the next few months were going to suck but I was determined to keep on plugging.

Little did I know that my time in the ER would reach out in my darkest hour and provide me with the most amazing possibility.

Go Pack!

The darkest days of my life were that first week unemployed. As you can imagine my decision wasn't that popular on the home front.

However, it was during this time that a warm, friendly hand reached out and tapped me on the shoulder and asked, "What are you doing tonight?"

The origin of this, the final story of the book began seven years before, when I worked at the small ritzy ER.

One day back then the Director asked, "Hey Dennis, do you mind interviewing an RN? She's in the consult room."

"Sure," I replied, "I'd be glad to."

It was winter and cold for San Antonio. The heating was having a hard time keeping up, so I wore long sleeves under my scrub top, and on my head, I wore a knitted Green Bay Packers winter cap.

As I stepped into the interview room, I said hello to Kimberly Geisler[94] who shook my hand, looked up at my hat and promptly blurted out, "Go Pack!"

---
[94] Now Zarobkiewicz

I laughed.

Kim added, "My family is from Wisconsin! In fact, I just recently moved down here from there."

I smiled and said, "Oh, that's awesome! My mom, dad, grandparents, everyone is from Wisconsin. The Northwoods to be exact."

We chatted about that for a while and then got down to business.

She was exactly what we were looking for.

Our time had ended, I shook her hand, thanked her for coming in and said, "Hang tight Kim, the director wants to come in and say hello."

She smiled and said, "Of course, no problem. It was so nice to meet you. Go Pack!"

I laughed and said, "Yeah, Go Pack! It was nice to meet you too."

I stepped out and closed the door behind me.

Well, I thought I had closed the door behind me. Turns out it was open about an inch.

At that moment the Director passed by and asked me, "What do you think of her? How did she do?"

Now, before I proceed let me first say that she was offered the job by us, but she didn't take it. She went to our health systems main hospital in the Medical Center. It was busier which is what she was looking for.

I eventually transferred over to that hospital about two years later and while there I saw Kim who I'd previously interviewed. We worked together for a little over a year in that ER before she moved on to the OR.

Anyway, the point is, that years later, when sitting around a table in the backyard at Kim's house enjoying some amazing BBQ prepared by her now husband Kuba, I learned, as Paul Harvey says, "The rest of the story."

So, it turns out that when Kim came to our hospital, it was the first interview in our city. She was a relatively new nurse, and this was her first time away from home.

In short, she was terrified and not sure she had what it would take to make it.

At the BBQ Kim told all of us around the table that when she came for the interview, she was full of doubt.

Her confidence level was quite low but when I stepped in with my Green Bay Packers hat on it immediately struck a chord. A commonality with someone so far from home. A wink from the universe.

Then, when I stepped out, I thought I had closed the door. On this night, at the BBQ, I learned that the door had actually not closed all the way and Kim could hear everything the director and I were saying.

The director asked, "What do you think of Kim? How did she do?"

I replied, "She did amazing. She's exactly what we're looking for. We'd be lucky to have her."

Sitting at the table I had tears in my eyes as Kim related how upon hearing those words she thought, "I got this! I can do this! People see my worth!"

Now, fast forward to the darkest time in my life. I'm unemployed and unsure of the future.

One day my phone rings and it's Kim, "Hey Kuba and I haven't seen you in a while and we're wondering if you want to meet us for dinner and catch up?"

"Heck yeah!" I exclaimed.

We met up and I explained to them everything that had happened. Including the fact that I was unemployed. I held nothing back.

I looked across the table and said, "Do you need a driver? I'm available."

They both laughed but then Kim shrugged her shoulders and said, "Actually, we might have something for you."

Kuba told me that he was thinking about starting another business but needed some research done. Would I be interested?

I jumped on it, "Absolutely!"

Kuba laughed and said, "Well, take a week and let me know what you think."

I knew right then the answer was yes, but I waited until the morning to let Kuba know that I was sure I wanted to work for him.

The position required me to do research. I could work from home and work the hours I wanted with a maximum of forty hours a week.

I laughed with delight. Wait, was this a dream? I could work from home in my shorts, work whatever hours I wanted, when I wanted. I had to pinch myself.

Well, that was a couple years ago and I'm still working with him.

To this day, from time to time, sitting around a table enjoying time with our friends and family, I'll look at them both and say, "Kuba, Kim, thank you for saving my life."

Clear!

The pages of this book cover a long span of my life. From that frozen hill in Iceland to the shattered computer glass in my last ER. I'm not special. There are people who've lived lives with much more extreme danger and excitement than mine. It's just that I've taken the time to write it down.

Perhaps God gives some of us that yearning to write because it's known that others may need to hear the story. Perhaps there's something about my journey that rings true in your own.

Just know you're not alone. There are others out there who feel the way you do. Dark. Alone. Angry. Sleep Deprived. Anxious. Depressed. Yet all the while saving lives. It's weird isn't it.

The character that makes us extremely good at helping others also kills us inside. Empathy. Compassion. Stewardship. We all have it, and it comes back around on us in the wee hours of the night, or on that drive home, with the music off, stuck in traffic. Watching people in their cars, wondering what they saw that day. What did they experience?

My story made many things clear to me, but it took me to the brink of annihilation to truly learn them. My battle with the Dark Passenger has been the toughest of my life. He's lost his power now, but I realize he's still there, lurking, watching for a moment of weakness. However, I vigilantly stand my ground, armed with tools provided by experts, the love of my family, friends, and a determination on my part that I will not disappear again.

Perhaps you will now understand that my most urgent hope for this book, is that you will read my story and find the strength to seek help. Help from professionals, not the bottle or pills. Those are only for the moment but even then, they only mask the true issues. I know.

Clear! Was the word I shouted when I warned my coworkers that I was about to deliver a shock to our patient. The hundreds of times I shouted this word all meant that things had gone poorly for a fellow human. It was an exclamation that things had become dire and that significant measures were being taken. It was a call for all hands to stand back and be Clear of the patient.

Clear! Was the fact that life is short so go to Alaska. Visit the New England States on a week-long tour. Go to that sibling you've not seen in a while and make things right. Ask out that person whose caught your heart and mind.

Clear! Is the fact that I did my best each and every shift, but it was not up to me whether my patients lived or died. I trained, practiced, and educated myself all to be the best for them, and I was. Then came the realization that I couldn't save them all, and that I had no control over who wore seat belts or who drove drunk. Bad things happen in this world, it's the price of free will.

Clear! Is the fact that the three hospitals I worked at devoted no time to the mental wellbeing of those on the front lines. Regarding the multitude of critical codes I worked in twenty-three years, I had a debriefing only one time. On paper these were supposed to happen each and every time, but they never did. Patient volume, staffing shortages and let's face it, money, were the reasons for this. This needs to change. In the ER we have devices like the glucometer and the Lifepak defibrillators that will get Quality Control checks run every single day. Yet, the humans? **Never!**

Clear! Is the fact that recently there have been tremendous breakthroughs in psychiatry dealing with PTSD. We've the veterans to thank for this and the tremendous strides the field of psychiatry has taken to truly grasp the workings of PTSD. Those of us in Emergency Medicine will benefit from the CRT program if only our hospital Chief Executive Officers and Chief Nursing Officers will demand it for their Emergency staff.

Clear! Is the fact that I worked with some of the most amazing, selfless, talented, compassionate, hilarious, and raunchy people on the planet. I loved them then and I love them now. PTSD drew me away from many of them, but they always have a special place in my heart reserved only for those of us who towed the line.

Clear! Is the fact that my family was immensely responsible for my ability to fight through the ravages of PTSD. Were it not for my girls I'm not sure I would still be here. I would not have survived but for my parent's constant support, literally picking me up off the street in the rain as I cried and cried taking advantage of the façade the rain provided to my cheeks.

Clear! Is the fact that I also owe my ability to draw breath to the amazing psych counselors I was fortunate enough to have. They were patient and gracious. They saved my life and changed my perspective, my reality.

Clear! Is the fact that each and every one of you deserves a full life. You deserve to pursue your dreams apart from your job, but you must seek help and put those ghosts to rest. I implore you to swallow that pride and get the help. Get the tools that will help you battle your own **Dark Passenger**. You'll be surprised to hear who around you suffer from the same issues.

Looking back at this time in my life, the events covered in this book, and the time span involved I could not help but marvel at all that I've seen. I'm thankful for the chance I had to help people and grateful that I can now see all these things and a new life, Crystal…Clear!

Printed in Great Britain
by Amazon